SWAPS

SWAPS

Second Edition

SHERREE DECOVNY

PRENTICE HALL EUROPE

London   New York   Toronto   Sydney   Tokyo
Singapore   Madrid   Mexico City   Munich   Paris

First published 1992 by Woodhead-Faulkner Ltd

Second edition published 1998
by Prentice Hall Europe
Campus 400, Maylands Avenue
Hemel Hempstead
Hertfordshire, HP2 7EZ

A division of Simon & Schuster International Group

Typeset in 10pt Caslon 224 Book
by Fakenham Photosetting Ltd, Fakenham, Norfolk

Printed and bound in Great Britain by T J International, Padstow, Cornwall

Library of Congress Cataloging-in-Publication Data available from the publisher

British Library Cataloguing in Publication Data

A catalogue record for this book is available from the British Library

ISBN 0-13-694258-X

2 3 4 5   02 01 00 99 98

CONTENTS

ACKNOWLEDGEMENTS

The author wishes to thank the International Swaps and Derivatives Association for supplying valuable data on the swaps market and the standard ISDA documentation. Furthermore, special thanks to Keith Redhead for reviewing the manuscript of the first edition of this book and for his suggestions for changes.

INTRODUCTION TO THE SWAP MARKET

1

In the early 1980s, interest rate and currency swaps were little known products used by select counterparties on rare occasions. However, over the years the market has experienced phenomenal growth, and swap products are now used worldwide by financial institutions and large corporate end users alike. This chapter will look at the development of the swap market and will examine some of the reasons for the growth in the market and the underlying rationale for swapping.

THE FINANCIAL MARKETS PRE-SWAPS

The development of parallel loans

Parallel loans were the forerunners of swaps, in particular currency swaps, and were popular in the late 1960s and 1970s as a means of financing investment abroad in the face of exchange control regulations. For example, if a company was conducting business in a foreign country with receipts generated in the foreign currency, the inability to convert the foreign currency freely into the domestic currency presented foreign exchange risk. Via the parallel loan, two companies based in different countries would borrow funds denominated in their own domestic currency. The two companies would then lend each other the funds denominated in their own domestic currency. In effect, it was like a swap except it was directly between two companies rather than using a bank or other financial institution as an intermediary.

There were three major problems with the parallel loans. First, if one party defaulted, the other party was not automatically released from its obligations under the loan agreement. Second, even though the two loans cancelled each other out, they were still considered on-balance sheet items for accounting and regulatory purposes. Third, parallel loans were difficult to arrange, because it was necessary to find two counterparties with exactly offsetting needs.

THE DEVELOPMENT OF THE SWAP MARKET

The swap market as we know it today has existed only since 1981, although some single examples can be found dating back to the mid-1970s. The earliest swaps were currency swaps and were developed to overcome some of the problems and complicated documentation procedures associated with parallel loans. These swaps were off-balance sheet transactions and involved no initial exchange of principal. If there was an initial exchange this consisted of a separate foreign exchange transaction.

A landmark in the development of the swap market was the IBM–World Bank swap in 1981. The international renown of the counterparties helped to impart a measure of popularity and acceptance that led to more activity in the market. In 1985 alone, the World Bank was engaged in 50 swaps with an average maturity of 6.4 years and a total principal amount of $1.36 billion. Of the total principal, $887 million was swapped into Swiss francs, $268 million into Deutschemarks, $96 million into guilders and $109 million into Japanese yen. The World Bank's swap transactions reduced the overall borrowing cost by 5.56%.[1]

The interest rate swap market developed as a means of arbitraging and utilizing relative credit advantages, utilizing differentials between the bond market and the short-term credit markets. In the early 1980s swaps were usually between a bank and a company, because banks found it relatively easier to raise fixed-rate finance and companies to raise floating-rate finance, while many corporate treasurers in fact preferred fixed-rate liabilities. At this time swaps were generally matched one-off deals.

Originally there were few companies and banks involved in the swaps market. Banks which did run a swaps book, did so on a 'matched' basis, thus the bank's role was as an intermediary (Figure 1.1). A swap was entered into only if an exact match was available on the other side. The bank's only risk was the credit risk of both parties. For the bank, this was a way of arbitraging, by effectively buying securities in one market and selling them simultaneously in another

FIGURE 1.1 The bank as an intermediary

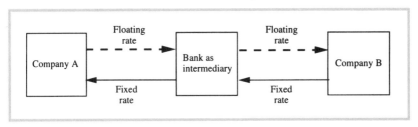

for a profit. The trouble with running a matched book, was that it was expensive, time consuming and it was difficult to find counterparties with interests to match exactly the original deal.

As a result, the swap market moved more towards the mismatched book approach. Banks, still wearing their intermediary hats, entered into swaps with different floating indices, different fixed-rate bases or different reset dates. Instead of necessarily matching swaps immediately, dealers began to act as the counterparty by taking the swap into its own warehouse until the swap could be matched at a later date. The banks would then hedge their portfolios with instruments such as futures and treasury bonds until the swaps could be offset. The ability for swap principals to warehouse swaps as well as innovative duration and zero coupon yield curve hedging techniques has led to a much greater degree of flexibility.

The dollar interest rate swap market was the first to develop a market away from matched deals. As banks developed hedging techniques they became able to enter into a swap with one counterparty and take out an offsetting hedge in the bond on the futures market until a matching swap could be found. These hedges might involve the mismatches listed above. Today there are a number of market-makers in interest rate swaps in many widely used currencies, although transactions in less popular currencies tend to be matched. The US dollar swap market is still the most active, but in recent years swaps in exotic currencies have played an increasingly significant role.

The swap market is now moving toward a more standardized product. Furthermore, with the growth in the market and a greater understanding of the swap product, participants are far less concerned with establishing a relationship with their bankers than they are in getting a good price and a quick execution.

CREDIT ARBITRAGE AND THE GROWTH OF THE SWAP MARKET

The cost of borrowing long-term funds can be broken down into four components: the risk-free rate which is set over the life of the instrument, the risk premium associated with the future uncertainty of the risk-free rate, the credit premium on the debt issued by a particular borrower, and the risk premium associated with a potential change in the credit premium of the borrower. When calculating the cost of borrowing by way of fixed-rate debt, floating-rate debt or short-term debt, credit premiums will be accounted for in a different manner. Fixed-rate debt fixes all the components, floating-rate debt fixes the credit spread but allows the risk-free rate to float, while short-term debt allows both the risk-free rate and the credit spread to float.[2] This section will concentrate on the credit spread component and its relevance to interest rate swaps.

Comparative advantage

The economic concept of comparative advantage is often applied to the rationale for swaps. Comparative advantage in this application is essentially that one company may be able to borrow funds at a comparatively lower rate than another company based on its credit standing. Through the swap market, firms are theoretically able to arbitrage the quality spread differential (QSD). A QSD is the premium a weaker credit must pay over a stronger credit when raising funds of the same denomination and maturity. As the maturity lengthens, the differential should widen reflecting the relationship between time and risk. Proponents of comparative advantage argue this has given a boost to the swap market, particularly the generic (fixed- versus floating-rate) swap market.

For example, if a US company has heavily issued bonds in the domestic market, domestic investors may require a premium to continue to purchase more of the firm's bonds. Therefore, the company may be able to raise funds at a more preferential rate in a foreign market where investors may be willing to purchase the company's bonds with a lower coupon. Thus, it is said that both the varying supply and demand for certain types of debt issues and issuers as well as the different criteria for credit quality analysis used in the international capital markets facilitated the growth in the swaps market.

Although the AAA firm can borrow funds more cheaply than the BBB firm in both the long-term and short-term markets, the AAA firm has a comparative advantage in the long-term market. The comparative advantage is calculated by listing the rates at which each party can borrow and netting them off. For example, if an AAA borrower can raise fixed-rate funds at 10% and floating-rate funds at LIBOR (London Interbank Offered Rate) + 0.25 and a BBB borrower can raise fixed-rate funds at 11.25% and floating-rate funds at LIBOR + 0.50, then the arbitrage is 1.00% (representing 1.25–0.25). Thus, in theory the savings is equal to the quality spread differential.

The argument behind comparative advantage rests on the assumption that the credit risk premium between a good credit and a poor credit is less on a floating-rate note than on a fixed-rate instrument.[3] This can be disputed in that the investor will be exposed to credit risk over a given period of time whether the underlying instrument is a floating-rate instrument or a fixed-rate instrument. In addition, the growth of the asset swap market keeps fixed and floating rates in line, particularly for weaker credits. It might be the case that a firm cannot raise funds in a foreign market cheaper than in the domestic market, because foreign investors may have to pay more for information about the firm.

Smith et al. note that any gain from arbitraging the swap market is illusory, as arbitrage eliminates any comparative advantage:

> *The problem with this argument, however, is that the very process of exploiting this kind of opportunity should soon eliminate it. The opening and expansion of a swap market effectively increases the demand for loans in low-rate markets and reduces the demand in higher-rate markets, thereby eliminating the supposed rate differences. Moreover, if this were the only economic basis for swaps, the benefits to one party would come at the expense of the other. Thus, in reasonably efficient and integrated world capital markets, it seems difficult to attribute the continuing growth of the swaps market simply to interest rate differences, and thus financial arbitrage among world capital markets.[4]*

Instead, Smith et al. propose that the growth in the swap market has been precipitated by the reduction in bid/offer spreads, the high demand by corporate users for instruments to manage interest rate risk, and the ability to use swaps to create synthetic financial instruments.

Quality spread differentials and shifting risk

Wall and Pringle have drawn on research done by Bierman and Hass and Jonkhart to show how the quality spread differential is partly based on the probability of bankruptcy:

> To illustrate, suppose that a BAA firm's probability of
> bankruptcy at some point during the next 10 years is 20 times
> that of its probability for next year, while a AAA firm's
> probability of bankruptcy over the next 10 years is only 11 times
> (or any number of greater than 10 and less than 20) its
> probability of failing next year. Both the BAA and the AAA firm
> will pay a greater risk premium on ten-year bonds than on one-
> year notes. However, the BAA will have to pay a proportionately
> greater risk premium because its risk of bankruptcy increases
> at a faster rate.[5]

Wall and Pringle draw on research done by Loeys to show that the
quality spread differential may be attributed to a shift in risk from a
firm's bondholders to its shareholders. When a firm funds itself by
issuing short-term debt, the debtholders have to wait only a relatively
short period of time before exercising the right not to renew the debt at
maturity if they perceive the firm to be more risky than when they first
bought the debt. On the other hand, if the firm has issued long-term
debt, the debtholders will have to wait a longer period of time before
making the decision whether to renew the obligation. If this is the case,
firms that are more reliant on short-term debt shift the longer-term
risk to the equity holders. Thus, companies that use short-term debt
should have higher equity capitalization rates than firms which issue
long-term debt. If a weaker credit firm issues short-term debt and
swaps this into long-term debt, the lower cost of funding is offset by the
higher equity capitalization rate. The stronger credit counterparty's
savings can be attributed to compensation for the credit risk.

Whether the bondholders or shareholders assume a greater risk is a
two-sided argument. One side of the argument is that if a company
with a weak credit rating issues long-term debt, then it is increasing
the risk of the firm at the expense of the bondholders. If the firm has
issued long-term debt and subsequently runs into financial distress,
then the management may be inclined to shift to higher-risk projects.
If these projects ultimately go wrong, the bondholders receive only the
promised rate of return, while at the same time they assume the risk
that they will lose all in the event of bankruptcy. On the other hand,
the shareholders receive any gains from the upside potential.

The other side of the argument is that, consequently, bondholders
require a larger premium on long-term debt issued by firms with
weaker credit ratings, which may cause the shareholders to suffer. If
the firm is making higher interest payments to the bondholders, there
will be less profit retained in the firm and fewer resources for
investment, potentially limiting future returns to the shareholders. In
other words, if the weaker credit firm issues long-term non-callable

debt, it is more inclined to shift investment from low-risk projects to high-risk projects, which eventually translates to higher payments to bondholders as a risk premium and lower retained earnings and providing the incentive to underinvest in the long run.

As Wall notes, the growth in the swap market may be attributed to agency costs.[6] Firms may be able to circumvent agency costs by issuing short-term floating-rate debt which would carry a lesser risk premium and swapping it to longer-term fixed-rate debt. Earlier it was stated that firms which issue short-term debt must offset this by a higher equity capitalization rate, and Jonkhart's model shows that while initially the cost of funding will be reduced, over time the firm's probability of bankruptcy will increase, and thus, so will the cost of short-term debt. While this strategy may work for borrowers who expect that the risk-free rates will increase but at the same time are optimistic about their own credit standing, some suggest that any gains are illusory. Wall argues that the swap would reduce the cost of funding providing a real, not illusory, saving without an increase in the equity capitalization rate. The reason is because the firm will not have the incentive to shift to high-risk projects and underinvest.

Quality spread differentials and embedded call options

Smith et al.'s theory is that some floating-rate agreements, as well as some fixed-rate agreements, carry an embedded call option or an option to prepay the debt, and because the call option is often overlooked, the credit risk is thus underpriced, giving rise to the quality spread differential. If the call option was taken into account, the differential in credit premium would disappear, and so would the comparative advantage argument as a motivation for swaps. They also argue that the gain from raising floating-rate funds combined with a swap, transforming the liability to a fixed-rate liability, can be attributed to the fact that the borrower's option to prepay – that is, the embedded call option – has been forfeited. In other words, as Wall and Pringle point out by drawing on the work by Smith et al., the present value of forfeiting the call option should be equal to the present value of the interest payments.

Smith et al. also note that because there are inherent differences in the practices of the US domestic market and the Eurobond market, the quality spread differential may appear to be larger than it actually is:

> Unlike domestic US issues, Eurobond debt contracts often
> adjust call prices for changes in market interest rates, thereby
> lowering the option value of the call provision. Thus the quality
> spread at the long end may be artificially inflated by comparing

rates paid on lower-rated debt issued in the US markets against higher-rated Eurobond issues.[7]

Swaps: a zero-sum game[8]

According to Stuart Turnbull, swaps are a zero-sum game if the bond markets for fixed- and floating-rate debt are competitive. Turnbull analyzed an interest rate swap from the point of view of Counterparty A (the receiver in the swap), the point of view of Counterparty B (the payer in the swap), as well as the financial intermediary's point of view to show that all parties are not in a position to benefit.

The basis of Turnbull's argument is that if Counterparty A is a stronger credit than Counterparty B, then the latter's cost of borrowing can be expressed as Counterparty A's cost of borrowing plus a differential. Suppose Counterparty A raises fixed-rate funds and Counterparty B raises floating-rate funds, and the two subsequently enter into an interest rate swap. The quality spread differential will be split between the two counterparties. In order for the swap to be beneficial to Counterparty A, the cost of participating in the swap must be less than the cost of issuing non-callable floating-rate debt directly. Likewise, for the swap to be beneficial to Counterparty B, the cost of participating in the swap must be less than the cost of issuing non-callable fixed-rate debt directly. For the swap to benefit the financial intermediary, the present value of its inflows must be greater than or equal to its outflows. Through a series of equations forming a proof, Turnbull concludes that a swap involves a shifting of risk amongst the counterparties, but unless there are externalities in the market, all the counterparties cannot gain from shifting risk.

TAX AND REGULATORY ARBITRAGE

The presence of government restrictions on capital flows or the pricing of capital flows has given rise to artificial differential pricing and differential access for different classes of capital market participants. As a result, the various participants have used the swap market to circumvent these restrictions.

Prior to the existence of the swap market, companies issuing dollar-denominated securities were subject to the stringent US securities regulations as well as the US tax code. In 1985, Loeys estimated that the cost of meeting Securities and Exchange Commission (SEC) requirements on a US dollar domestic long-term bond issue translated to approximately an 80 basis point premium over a comparable

Eurodollar issue.[9] Once the currency swap market came into existence, capital market participants came to enjoy a greater degree of flexibility. The firm could achieve a saving by issuing a Eurobond combined with a swap. The company could issue a bond in yen, for example, and thus be subject to the more favourable Japanese tax code while still swapping the exposure back to US dollars.

Therefore, in addition to credit criteria and supply and demand, different tax and regulatory structures also contributed to the growth of the swap market. There are several motives for a market participant to use the swap market to take advantage of tax and regulatory arbitrage. For instance, the firm may be seeking a way to circumvent legislation on withholding tax or tax differentials. Alternatively, the fund manager or treasurer may be seeking a way to circumvent internal restrictions imposed by the firm or change the structure of a subsidized loan.

Withholding tax and tax differentials

It is natural for investors to seek to maximize after tax income while borrowers will seek to minimize after tax costs of funding. Withholding tax and tax differentials give rise to arbitrage, because their presence translates into a financial difference between securities held in the domestic market and securities held in other markets such as the Eurobond market. The various types of income or expense may be treated differently for tax purposes depending on the category or perspective of the investor or borrower.

For example, in some countries, such as Australia, if a foreigner owns domestic bonds, then the interest payments on the bonds are subject to tax. A tax credit might be claimed on the tax return in the home country, depending on the tax domicile of the bondholder, but this inevitably causes delays in the bondholder receiving his or her money and could result in some loss in yield. This situation gave a big boost to the growth of the Eurobond market on the demand side, because investors could pick up yield through not being liable for tax. The demand is met, because borrowers have the flexibility to raise funds in the Eurobond market and swap into another currency or interest rate structure. The key to the success of this strategy on the supply side is that swap payments and receipts are not usually subject to withholding tax. Moreover, a hedging transaction may be taxed on a more preferential basis than a speculative transaction. Thus, the growth of the Eurobond market can largely be attributed to the desire on the part both of the borrowers and of the investors to defer or avoid income taxes. This is discussed in more detail in Chapters 4 and 6.

Internal investment restrictions

It is not uncommon for corporate policy-makers to impose internal restrictions on the types of products which will be used for borrowing or investment. Fund managers, for example, are often restricted from using futures and options, and when launching issues, treasurers may be restricted on the denomination of the funds being raised. In both cases, the swap market provides a way of circumventing these restrictions, and any cost advantage is able to be utilized as the basis for swap arbitrage.

For example, until the mid-1980s under Japanese tax law, zero-coupon bonds were not taxable until maturity, and at that stage they were taxed at the capital gains rate which was a favourable rate. In addition, the investment portfolios of pension funds were limited to no more than 10% of non-yen denominated bonds issued by foreign corporations. US corporations took advantage of this legislation by doing two issues. The first issue was a zero-coupon bond denominated in yen, which enabled the investors to take advantage of the lower capital gains tax and the deferral of the actual payment of tax. The second issue was a dual currency bond which paid interest in yen and repaid the principal in dollars. The dual currency bond qualified as a yen-denominated issue even though by virtue of its structure it was really a dollar zero, thus enabling the Japanese pension funds to circumvent the 10% limit while internationally diversifying their portfolios. At the same time, the firm was able to pair the bond issue with a currency swap to change their exposure to a dollar one and reduce their cost of funding.

Furthermore, the 10% quota imposed by the Japanese Ministry of Finance did not count non-yen denominated bonds issued by Japanese resident companies. In this way, Japanese banks were able to satisfy the investor demand for non-yen denominated securities by issuing bonds denominated in Australian dollars, which at the time carried relatively high yields, at a lower yield than a domestic Australian dollar issue. The Japanese banks were able to enter into a swap with an Australian domestic counterparty, changing the exposure to a US dollar one while at the same time lowering its cost of funds.

Subsidized funding sources

Some borrowers may be in a position to take advantage of subsidized funding sources. For example, an exporter may be eligible for an ECGD loan for the purchase of underlying capital goods, but the borrower may want to change the denomination of the loan or the interest rate structure to suit a specific project. In this case, if the borrower combines the loan with a swap, the borrower may use its comparative advantage to lower its overall cost of funding while enjoying the flexibility of changing the structure of the loan.

SWAP VOLUMES AND GROWTH OF THE MARKET

The size of the interest rate and currency swap market increased twenty-fold between 1987 and 1995 (see Table 1.1). The 1995 International Swap Dealers Association's (ISDA) survey of 80 member organizations shows that transactions outstanding in interest rate swaps, currency swaps and interest rate options at the close of 1995 stood at $17.713 trillion in notional principal, up 56.7% from 11.303 trillion at year-end 1994. Based on information provided by participating swaps dealers in Asia, Australia, Europe and North America, there were 430,842 swaps transactions of all types outstanding at the close of 1995, compared with 306,197 at the same point a year earlier.

The survey found that the total of outstandings in the second half of 1995 climbed 27.2% from the first half of the year: 18.4% for interest rate swaps, 15.2% for currency swaps and 79.3% for interest rate options. The aggregate notional principal of new business activity in 1995 rose 37.3% to $11.169 trillion from the previous year's $8,133 trillion.

For interest rate swaps, which dominate activity in privately negotiated derivatives, year-end outstandings increased 45.3% to $12.811 trillion from $8.816 trillion at the close of 1994 and 18.4% from $10,817 trillion at mid-year 1995. The notional volume of new business for 1995 grew 39.4% to $8.699 trillion, compared to 1994's $6,241 trillion. Second-half activity amounted to $5.270 trillion, up 53.7% from $3,429 trillion in the preceding six months.

Interest rate options (caps, collars, floors and swaptions) that were outstanding at year-end 1995 stood at $3.704 trillion compared with $2.066 trillion at mid-year and $1,573 trillion a year earlier, a gain of 136% for the full year and 79.3% for the second half. New transactions in interest rate options grew 33.2% to $2.015 trillion from $1.513 trillion. Activity in the second half amounted to $1.340 trillion, almost double the $675.8 billion volume of activity in the first six months.

Currency swaps also registered gains. Contracts outstanding at the close of 1995 amounted to $1.197 trillion, up 15.1% from $1.040 trillion at mid-year and up 30.9% from $914.8 billion at the close of 1994. Activity in currency swaps for the full 12 months of 1995 totalled $455.1 billion, a 20% increase over $379.3 billion in the

TABLE 1.1 ISDA market survey summary statistics (in billions of dollars)

	INTEREST RATE SWAPS		CURRENCY SWAPS		INTEREST RATE OPTIONS		TOTAL OF ALL ACTIVITY	
	ACTIVITY	OUTSTANDINGS	ACTIVITY	OUTSTANDINGS	ACTIVITY	OUTSTANDINGS	ACTIVITY	OUTSTANDINGS
1H87	181.5		43.5				225.0	
2H87	206.3	682.8	42.3	182.8			248.6	865.6
1H88	250.5		60.3				310.8	
2H88	317.6	1,010.2	62.3	316.8		327.3	379.9	1,654.3
1H89	389.2		77.6		186.8		653.6	
2H89	444.4	1,502.6	92.0	434.8	148.7	537.3	685.1	2,474.7
1H90	561.5		94.6		138.0		794.1	
2H90	702.8	2,311.5	118.1	577.5	154.3	561.3	975.2	3,450.3
1H91	762.1		161.3		198.8		1,122.2	
2H91	859.7	3,065.1	167.1	807.2	183.9	577.2	1,210.7	4,449.5
1H92	1,318.3		156.1		293.6		1,768.0	
2H92	1,504.3	3,850.8	145.8	860.4	298.8	634.5	1,948.9	5,345.7
1H93	1,938.4		156.8		509.7		2,604.9	
2H93	2,166.2	6,177.3	138.4	899.6	607.3	1,397.6	2,911.9	8,474.5
1H94	3,182.9		181.0		850.2		4,214.1	
2H94	3,058.0	8,815.6	198.3	914.8	663.0	1,572.8	3,919.3	11,303.2
1H95	3,428.9	10,817.0	153.8	1,039.7	675.8	2,066.2	4,258.5	13,922.9
2H95	5,269.9	12,810.7	301.3	1,197.4	1,339.6	3,704.5	6,910.8	17,712.6

Source: International Swaps and Derivatives Association.

previous year. Second-half activity nearly doubled to $301.3 billion from $153.8 billion in the first half.

To realize the effects of translating the survey's results into US dollars for reporting purposes, ISDA analysed historical survey data results, applying constant exchange rates. This analysis eliminates the portion of the reported increase due to a change in exchange rates and indicates the growth attributable to the increased volume in that particular transaction type in the currency. Based on constant exchange rates and using year-end 1995 exchange rates, the out-standings reported by ISDA for interest rate and currency swaps totalled $13.657 trillion versus the outstandings for interest rate and currency swaps of $14.008 trillion. The difference between the total outstanding numbers for 1995 was 2.57%.

However, the results reported by individual currencies between 1991 and 1995 differed substantially when analysed individually. Outstanding currency and interest rate swap transactions in Japanese yen were reported as having grown 369.8% between 1991 and 1995. In constant exchange rate terms, the growth was 278.9%. Other curren-cies where the reported growth rates and constant exchange rate growth rates differed included Deutschemark currency and interest rate swap outstandings, which grew 363.8% in constant exchange rate terms (versus the reported 400.9% growth) between 1991 and 1995. Transactions in other currencies also showed differences but did not have an impact on the overall reported numbers, because they represented a small percentage of the market.

Table 1.2 shows that interest rate swaps transactions in US dollars accounted for 34% of the year-end outstandings and 33% of the full year's activity. Currencies other than the US dollar accounted for the remaining two-thirds of the world's interest rate swaps activity and outstandings. Next to the US dollar swaps market, the Japanese yen swaps market was the most active with 26% of all activity in interest rate swaps, followed by the French franc (13%) and the Deutschemark (11%).

Preliminary data from ISDA's 1996 survey indicates that the combined notional amount of globally outstanding interest rate swaps, currency swaps and interest rate options grew by 37.1% from the end of 1995 to the close of 1996. Outstanding contracts stood at $24.292 trillion on 31 December 1996.

THE PLAYERS

In 1986, Wall and Pringle initiated a survey of swap users. The survey was based on a search of the National Automated Accounting Research

TABLE 1.2 1995 year-end swaps outstandings (US$ in millions)

| | Interest Rate Swaps | | | | | Currency Swaps | | | |
Currency	1995 YE ($)	1994 YE ($)	Diff %	As % of Total		1995 YE ($)	1994 YE ($)	Diff %	As % of Total
US dollar	4,371,650	3,230,056	35.3	34.1		418,883	321,553	30.3	35.0
Australian dollar	167,687	148,479	12.9	1.3		45,076	37,026	21.7	3.8
Belgian franc	74,631	50,618	47.4	0.6		10,359	8,000	29.5	0.9
British pound	853,977	674,025	26.7	6.7		45,749	42,993	6.4	3.8
Canadian dollar	219,714	224,467	−2.1	1.7		49,977	44,858	11.4	4.2
Danish krone	45,678	18,834	142.5	0.4		4,464	2,529	76.5	0.4
Deutschemark	1,438,884	911,670	57.8	11.2		119,008	76,941	54.7	9.9
Dutch guilder	101,846	56,975	78.8	0.8		14,039	9,190	52.8	1.2
ECU	223,149	163,493	36.5	1.7		49,500	27,398	51.5	3.5
Franch franc	1,219,875	461,655	164.2	9.5		40,693	24,499	66.1	3.4
Hong Kong dollar	39,971	21,411	86.7	0.3		4,122	2,483	66.0	0.3
Italian lira	405,402	259,548	56.2	3.2		36,312	25,631	41.7	3.0
Japanese yen	2,895,871	1,987,377	45.7	22.6		200,010	169,933	17.7	16.7
New Zealand dollar	6,063	5,484	10.6	0.0		1,517	2,015	−24.7	0.1
Spanish peseta	163,662	99,295	64.8	1.3		13,739	16,869	−18.6	1.1
Swedish krone	93,751	147,332	−36.4	0.7		16,490	18,645	−11.6	1.4
Swiss franc	331,676	201,666	64.5	2.6		75,286	63,607	18.4	6.3
Other currencies	157,249	153,176	2.7	1.2		60,170	20,715	190.5	5.0
Totals	12,810,736	8,815,561	45.3	100.0		1,205,394	914,885	30.9	100.0

Source: International Swaps and Derivatives Association.

System (NAARS) database of corporate annual reports maintained by the American Institute of Certified Public Accountants in New York. At the time the database consisted of 4,000 firms from the New York Stock Exchange, American Stock Exchange, Over-The-Counter companies that were on the Federal Reserve's list of stocks eligible for margin, the Fortune 500 and Fortune 500 corporations. After applying specific criteria, this list produced 250 US firms using swaps.[10]

The survey showed that 28.8% of swap users were commercial banks, 25.6% were non-financial and non-manufacturing firms, 21.6% were manufacturing firms, 14.8% were thrift institutions, and 9.2% were other financial institutions. The companies were broken down into categories of credit rating and categories of dealers, fixed-rate payers, floating-rate payers, both fixed- and floating-rate payers at one time or another, and those whose position could not be determined from the annual accounts. Of these companies, 50.8% were known to be fixed-rate payers. Of the fixed-rate payers with bonds outstanding, 86% were rated A+ or lower, whereas 50% of the floating-rate payers were rated AA− or better.

ISDA's 1995 survey reveals that the two main centres for interest rate swaps trading are the US and Europe, but Europe is playing a more prominent role. Table 1.3 shows that in 1995, 36% of interest rate swaps were traded in North America, while 46% of interest rate swaps were traded in Europe in 1995. Only 14% were traded in Asia, and 4% in other countries.

The ISDA 1995 survey also breaks down activity by business type. Of the 36% traded in North America, 9% of single currency interest rate swaps were traded by corporates, 16% by banks, 3% by institutional investors, 6% by governments, and 3% by other entities. In Europe, corporates accounted for 8% of interest rate swaps, while banks accounted for 31%. European institutional investors and governments each accounted for 2% of the volume, while other entities accounted for 3%. In Asia, corporates and banks each accounted for 6% of the total, while institutional investors and governments each accounted for 1%.

In the currency swap market, corporates as end users make up 32% of the swaps traded based on notional principal, as shown in Table 1.4. Banks make up 37%, institutional investors make up 6%, governments make up 21% and other entities make up 4%. The currency swap market is mainly centred in Europe, accounting for 55% of the outstanding swaps. Asia and North America follow, with a 22% and 20% share respectively. Outstanding swaps in other countries represent only 3% of the total.

Nonetheless, swaps have emerged as a flexible interest rate and currency risk management tool which can be used by bank treasuries,

TABLE 1.3 Interest rate swaps

Non-ISDA business/location analysis
Total notional principal (US $ equivalent) by percentage
1995 year end outstandings

| | | BUSINESS TYPE | | | |
LOCATION	CORPORATE (%)	BANKS (%)	INSTITUTIONAL INVESTORS (%)	GOVERNMENT ENTITIES (%)	OTHER (%)	TOTAL (%)
North America	9	16	3	6	3	36
Europe	8	31	2	2	3	46
Asia	6	6	1	1	0	14
Other	1	1	1	0	1	4
Total	24	53	7	9	7	100

Please note: The above matrix may not foot or cross-foot due to immaterial rounding differences.
All data shown for transactions between ISDA members has been divided by two to eliminate double counting.

Source: International Swaps and Derivatives Association.

TABLE 1.4 Currency swaps

Non-ISDA business/location analysis
Total notional principal (US $ equivalent) by percentage
1995 year end outstandings

LOCATION	CORPORATE (%)	BANKS (%)	INSTITUTIONAL INVESTORS (%)	GOVERNMENT ENTITIES (%)	OTHER (%)	TOTAL (%)
			BUSINESS TYPE			
North America	9	4	2	5	1	20
Europe	13	24	2	13	3	55
Asia	9	7	1	3	1	22
Other	1	1	0	1	0	3
Total	32	37	6	21	4	100

Please note: The above matrix may not foot or cross-foot due to immaterial rounding differences. All data shown for transactions between ISDA members has been divided by two to eliminate double counting.

Source: International Swaps and Derivatives Association.

building societies and savings and loans, insurance companies, pension funds, sovereigns, supranationals and corporate users.

For example, US thrifts and savings and loans tend to borrow short-term floating rate funds from their depositors and lend long-term fixed rate funds for mortgages. In this respect, they have a comparative advantage which they are able to exploit through the swaps market while managing their interest rate risk. A savings and loan might hedge its floating-rate funding cost by purchasing a pool of fixed-rate mortgages. It may then enter into a swap to pay the fixed rate and receive the floating rate. The floating-rate payments received on the swap will net off with the floating rate payable to its depositors, while the mortgage pool will serve as an effective hedge on the savings and loan's fixed-rate obligation under the swap.

For corporate end users, the swaps market serves as a means of asset and liability management. Swaps may be used to hedge an asset or to transform a liability, and they can be a useful instrument for corporate treasurers wishing to spread their risk between fixed-rate and floating-rate debt. The ability to obtain a fixed rate of interest on floating-rate debt through a swap can be useful for companies wishing to issue fixed-rate debt but without the credit rating to issue cost-effective long-term debt. Currency swaps can be a useful instrument for companies wishing to finance foreign investment or alter their financing structure in accordance with changed exchange rate horizons. The fact that interest rate swaps are reversible enables a degree of flexibility in management, and moreover, they may be entered into at short notice and with few or no transaction costs.

SUMMARY

The swap market developed out of an earlier product called a parallel or back-to-back loan. The trouble with this early product was that it carried a higher default risk, it was an on-balance sheet item, because money was physically being borrowed and lent, and it was difficult to arrange. However, the concept survived and a new and improved product emerged. Currency swaps were first to appear on the scene, but over the years interest rate swaps have become more widely used. The huge demand for the new product introduced a new dimension to bank intermediation, and now banks are able to warehouse swaps while managing their risks using various sophisticated techniques.

Academics have puzzled over the reasons for such spectacular growth in the swap market. One reason which is often cited as a rationale for entering into swaps is credit arbitrage and comparative advantage leading to a quality spread differential. Wall and Pringle summarize the four reasons for QSD arbitrage.[11] They are differences in the discounted value of expected bankruptcy costs, differences in the risk carried by the shareholders, differences in restrictive covenants and options, and agency costs. They claim that while the first three factors may give rise to a quality spread differential, they are not exploitable for economic gain, for any apparent gains through swaps or otherwise are illusory. Only the agency cost argument poses real gains. Therefore, only a percentage of the QSD stated in basis point is exploitable for economic gains.

Moreover, Smith et al. argue that if an opportunity exists for arbitrage, then an efficient market will soon eliminate it. Stuart Turnbull concludes that the traditional method of evaluating the benefits of swaps may be misleading. He has argued that it is impossible to arbitrage quality spread differentials, and that QSDs exist because of various factors which cannot be exploited for economic gain. Thus, swaps are really a zero-sum game – that is, where one party gains the other loses – without the presence of market imperfections and swap externalities.[12]

While the exploitation of credit arbitrage has often been discredited by academics, there are still many benefits that can be gained by using interest rate and currency swaps for asset and liability management. Wall and Pringle have noted that while there are several different, and often contradictory, theories accounting for the growth in the swap market, the absence of a formal market in interest rate swaps and the confidentiality of the deals makes monitoring and evaluating transactions and users extremely difficult. They suggest that it may be possible to glean some information from companies' annual reports and accounts; however, the treatment of swaps is not standard in this situation.[13]

Tax and regulatory arbitrage are often cited as motives for transacting swaps. Both borrowers and investors try to avoid withholding tax as it erodes real returns, and debt issues combined with swaps are often a way of circumventing tax. Swaps may also be used to circumvent internal company or government restrictions on the methods of raising finance or the currencies in which finance may be raised. Finally, some borrowers are eligible for preferential loans, so that their superior borrowing capacity may be used to an advantage in conjunction with swaps.

Notes

1. Fuad A. Abdullah and Virginia L. Bean. 'At last, a swaps primer', *Financial Executive*, vol. 4, July/August 1988, p. 56.

2. Marcelle Arak et al. 'Interest rate swaps: an alternative explanation', *Financial Management*, vol. 17, summer 1988, p. 15.

3. The credit risk premium on a floating-rate note is usually a fixed mark-up over a risk-free rate such as Treasury Bills.

4. Clifford W. Smith, Jr., Charles W. Smithson and Lee Macdonald Wakeman. 'The evolving market for swaps', *Midland Corporate Finance Journal*, winter 1986, p. 24.

5. Larry D. Wall and John J. Pringle. 'Alternative explanations of interest rate swaps: a theoretical and empirical analysis', *Financial Management*, vol. 18, summer 1989, p. 61.

6. See Marcelle Arak et al., op. cit. p. 14; and Larry D. Wall and John J. Pringle, op. cit., pp. 62–3.

7. Larry D. Wall and John J. Pringle, op. cit., p. 62.

8. For more detail see Stuart M. Turnbull, 'Swaps: a zero sum game?', *Financial Management*, spring 1987, pp. 15–22.

9. Larry D. Wall and John J. Pringle, op. cit., p. 64.

10. For a detailed discussion see Larry D. Wall and John J. Pringle, op. cit., pp. 65–8, 71–3.

11. Larry D. Wall and John J. Pringle, op. cit., p. 64.

12. See Larry D. Wall and John J. Pringle, op. cit., p. 60.

13. ibid.

Bibliography

Abdullah, Fuad A. and Bean, Virginia L. (1988). 'At last, a swaps primer', *Financial Executive*, vol. 4, July/August pp. 53–7.

Antl, Boris (ed.) (1986). *Swap Finance, Vols I and II*. London: Euromoney Publications Ltd.

Arak, Marcelle et al. (1988). 'Interest rate swaps: an alternative explanation', *Financial Management*, vol. 17, summer, pp. 12–18.

Das, Satyaiit (1989). *Swap Financing*. London: IFR Publishing Ltd.

DeCovny, Sherree and Tacchi, Christine (1991). *Hedging Strategies*. Cambridge: Woodhead-Faulkner (Publishers) Ltd.

Durr, Barbara (1991). 'Chicago looks to a new future', *Financial Times*, 21 June, p. 27.

Hamilton, James (1990). 'An introduction to swap products', *The Treasurer*, vol. 12, no. 2, February, pp. 6–9.

International Swap Dealers Association, Inc. and Arthur Andersen & Co. (1995). 'Market Survey Highlights, Year End 1995'.

Smith, Donald J. (1988). 'Measuring the gains from arbitraging the swap market', *Financial Executive*, vol. 4, March/April, pp. 46–9.

Smith Jr., Clifford W., Smithson, Charles W. and Macdonald Wakeman, Lee (1986). 'The evolving market for swaps', *Midland Corporate Finance Journal*, winter, pp. 20–32.

Turnbull, Stuart M. (1987). 'Swaps: a zero sum game?', *Financial Management*, spring, pp. 15–22.

Wall, Larry D. and Pringle, John J. (1989). 'Alternative explanations of interest rate swaps: a theoretical and empirical analysis', *Financial Management*, vol. 18, summer, pp. 59–73.

INTEREST RATE SWAPS 2

The generic swap is perhaps the most commonly used swap product. In this chapter, the mechanics of the generic interest rate swap will be discussed including the methods of pricing, valuing and hedging swaps. Once the reader has mastered these basic principles, they can easily be applied to other structures discussed later on in the book.

DESCRIPTION OF GENERIC/PLAIN VANILLA INTEREST RATE SWAPS

The most commonly used interest rate swap is called a 'generic' or 'plain vanilla' swap. The plain vanilla swap involves an agreement between parties to exchange periodic payments calculated on the basis of a specified coupon rate and a mutually agreed notional principal amount. Plain vanilla swaps are typically an exchange of floating-rate interest obligations for fixed-rate interest obligations. The counterparties in the swap are known as the payer of the fixed rate and the receiver of the fixed rate. Thus, one may think of a plain vanilla swap as a notional loan and deposit in the same currency, principal amount and maturity. Alternatively, the payer of the swap is effectively short a fixed-rate security and long a floating-rate security, while the receiver is short a floating-rate security and long a fixed-rate security.

Interest rate swaps can be arranged for any length of time and notional principal amount, although active trading tends to take place only up to 10 years. Larger amounts and longer periods tend to be restricted in availability due to market liquidity and credit requirements. In particular, swap counterparties have become more credit sensitive. This is discussed in more detail in Chapter 6.

Quotations for interest rate swaps in a required currency can be obtained from the major commercial and investment banks in major financial centres. On-line services such as Reuters and Telerate provide a screen quotation service from money brokers and some banks. These screens are not a live dealing service, but provide indicative quotations and can be useful to potential users monitoring the market before implementing a hedge using a swap product. Prior to entering into a swap transaction, it is advisable to obtain a quotation from a few market-makers, since quotations may vary according to the market-maker's position.

Figure 2.1 shows an example of a plain vanilla or generic swap. The principal is $10 million, the life of the swap is 5 years. In this example, Counterparty A is the fixed-rate payer. Counterparty A has borrowed floating-rate funds but wants to pay interest at a fixed rate. On the other hand, Counterparty B is the fixed-rate receiver. Counterparty B has borrowed fixed-rate funds but sees interest rates declining and decides to swap some of this fixed-rate borrowings for floating rate. An interest rate swap can thus be used to transform one type of interest rate obligation into another enabling the participants to adjust their interest rate obligations to meet their needs in a particular rate environment and hedge against future changes in rates or lock in a profit margin.

The only exchange that is made is interest payments on the principal, whereas payments corresponding to the principal amounts are not involved in the transaction. In fact, the principal could already have been invested, for instance, in plant and equipment.

FIGURE 2.1   A generic/plain vanilla swap: $10 million 5 years

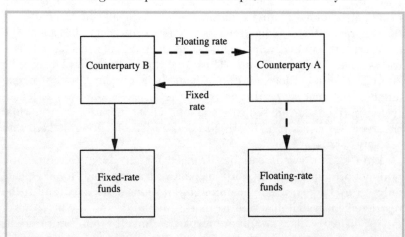

Besides the generic or plain vanilla swap, there are several other structures of interest rate swaps. Some examples include basis swaps, amortizing and roller-coaster swaps, off-market coupon swaps, LIBOR-in-arrears swaps, participation swaps and zero-coupon swaps. In the majority of fixed/floating interest rate swaps, the floating rate used is based on LIBOR (London Interbank Offered Rate) but other bases for floating interest rates such as Treasury Bills, US Prime, Fed Funds and Commercial Paper can be used. These structures will be covered in detail in Chapter 5.

HOW A SWAP IS TRANSACTED

A swap transaction is normally carried out by telephone, and the deal is closed when the coupon rate, the floating-rate basis, the day basis, the start date, the maturity date, rollover dates, the governing law and the documentation are agreed. The transaction is confirmed immediately by telex or fax followed by a written confirmation, but the stage at which the deal becomes binding is the moment of agreement on the telephone.

Documentation in the major money centres is usually based on the International Swaps and Derivatives Association (ISDA) format. The documentation is of a standard format with a number of optimal clauses to suit individual cases. ISDA documentation has two major parts, the master agreement which can cover all future agreements between the two counterparties, and the attached confirmation of the deal in question. This is discussed in more detail in Chapter 6. At the time of dealing the swap, it is agreed which of the two counterparties will draw up the documents. First, a draft copy is exchanged, and when all details are agreed the final documents are exchanged and signed by the authorized signatories. Future deals between the two counterparties can then be concluded by a confirmation only which is attached to the original master agreement.

SWAPS PRICING

There are four main components of a swap price. They are a benchmark price, supply and demand (usually relating to bonds or futures), transaction costs (such as origination fees and financing costs), and credit risk (the probability that the counterparty will default).

Swap rates are based on a series of benchmark instruments in the treasury bond markets. They may also be quoted as a spread over the yield on these benchmark instruments as well as on an absolute interest rate basis. For example, if one is quoted a 5-year swap rate of 8.28% and the 5-year treasury note is yielding 7.73%, then the spread over the treasury note is 55 basis points. The 55 basis points will be made up of all of the rest of the factors listed above.

Supply and demand factors will affect the pricing of a swap. For example, depending on the market-maker's book, the size of the principal amount will affect how aggressive the market-maker will be in pricing a swap. Moreover, the market-maker is likely to be more aggressive if the swap structure is easy to lay off in the market. For example, many banks dealing in US dollar swaps prefer the floating-rate index to be against 6-month or 3-month LIBOR rather than the prime rate, and thus will be more aggressive in quoting a price for the former.

Liquidity, which is a function of supply and demand, plays an important role in swaps pricing. In particular, if there are few participants in the market, the swap user is less likely to be able to convert the swap position into cash. In illiquid markets, a large transaction may have a disproportionate impact on the market. Consequently, in illiquid markets, bid/offer spreads are normally wider.

Transaction costs and credit risk must also be built into the swap price. Transaction costs occur when a swap is done in conjunction with a new issue. Fees and expenses which may run at approximately 2.25% of the principal amount may be amortized over the life of the swap, contributing to the all-in price of the swap. In addition, if the swap is arranged through a money broker, the broker will charge an up-front fee of approximately 1 basis point per annum discounted at the swap rate. Credit risk must be accounted for in swaps pricing to reflect the probability that the counterparty will default. Moreover, if a Counterparty A wishes to assign the swap, a third party must be able to accept the credit of Counterparty B.

Interest rate swaps are normally quoted as a fixed rate of interest per annum payable on a principal amount. When dealing a swap the parties involved must take care to state on which basis the swap is being dealt. The basis is usually referred to as bond basis or money market basis; however, these terms alone can be misleading. Money market basis implies that interest payments are calculated on an A/360 basis, but bond basis can mean A/365, 30/360 or even 360/360.[1] Furthermore, swaps may be dealt on an annual, semi-annual or quarterly basis. The following is a list of the most commonly used bases for swaps in the major currencies:

British pound	A/365	Deutschemark	30/360
Belgian franc	A/365	ECU	30/360
Japanese yen	A/365	Guilder	30/360
Australian dollar	A/365	Italian lira	30/360
Swiss franc	30/360		
US dollar	A/360 or A/365		

Sterling interest rate swaps, for example, are normally payable semi-annually against receiving 6-month sterling LIBOR. However, it is normally possible to arrange for any combinations of annual/semi-annual/quarterly interest payments on both the fixed and floating sides of the swap. US dollar interest rate swaps are usually quoted as annual or semi-annual money market or annual or semi-annual bond.

When evaluating the benefits of a swap in conjunction with an asset or liability, it is imperative to equate the interest rate basis; otherwise, what appears to be a significant gain may actually be an illusion. If a rate is quoted on an annual basis, but one needs to know the rate on another basis, the rate can quickly be approximated by using the following equations:

To change from semi-annual to annual: $\text{rate} + (\text{rate}^2 \div 400)$

To change from annual to semi-annual: $\text{rate} - (\text{rate}^2 \div 400)$

To change from semi-annual to quarterly:
$$\sqrt[2]{(\text{rate} \div 200 + 1)} - 1 \times 400$$

To change from quarterly to semi-annual:
$$(\text{rate} \div 400 + 1)^2 - 1 \times 200$$

To change from annual to quarterly:
$$\sqrt[4]{(\text{rate} \div 100 + 1)} - 1 \times 400$$

It is worth noting that with few exceptions, including sterling, LIBOR is quoted on a 360-days-in-the-year basis, whereas bonds are often quoted on the basis of a 365-day year. Therefore, when comparing LIBOR to bond yields, it is necessary to multiply LIBOR by 365/360.

Swap spreads

There are several factors which influence swap spreads, including the cost of carry of the hedge instrument, supply and demand, credit arbitrage (which was discussed at length in Chapter 1), the shape of the yield curve and movement in the treasury markets. Moreover, the determination of swap spreads will depend on the currency of the swap. While the US dollar swaps market is closely linked to the actively traded US treasury market, swaps denominated in other currencies may be more closely linked to other factors.

As a basis for a swap spread it is necessary to look at the cost of carry of the hedge instrument. In the US dollar market, swaps are priced as a spread over treasuries, and an active repo market exists for financing hedge positions. Later in the chapter, it will be explained that the payer in the swap will hedge the position by buying treasuries and the receiver in the swap will hedge the position by selling treasuries. From the payer's point of view, the treasuries purchased are likely to be financed through the repo market. A look at the cash flows will show that the payer in the swap is receiving LIBOR and receiving a coupon payment on the treasuries while paying the repo rate on the treasuries. The net carry on the hedge plus LIBOR will provide the absolute rate on the swap bid side. As swaps are priced as a spread over treasuries, the absolute rate on the swap minus the yield on the treasury note equals the spread. Put more simply:

Swap spread
= [LIBOR + (treasury coupon − repo rate)] − treasury yield

For example, the coupon on the 5-year treasury note is 7.625 currently yielding 7.738, the repo rate is 5.75 and LIBOR is 6.375. The absolute rate on the bid side of the swap will be 8.25 which is 51 basis points over the 5-year treasury note. Bid/offer spreads in the US dollar swap market are normally 5 to 10 basis points, so the offered side will be 56 to 61 basis points over the treasury note.

Supply and demand factors will often influence the direction of swap spreads. As the swap market is heavily linked to the Eurobond market, the number of issues being launched can have an effect on spreads. For example, if there are many issues in the market which are being swapped from a fixed-rate liability to a floating-rate liability by the borrowers, then a demand for swap payers will be created. As a result, swaps spreads can drift lower unless there is sufficient demand on the bid side. Likewise, a change in perception of the riskiness of a currency could push spreads higher. If foreign receivers expect the US dollar to fall, then they will require a higher spread over treasuries to compensate for anticipated losses on the currency.

A rally in the treasury market could have the effect of pushing spreads higher. When interest rates fall sharply, corporations often want to fix their borrowing costs by swapping floating-rate liabilities into fixed-rate liabilities. The abundance of swap payers and demand for swap receivers would put upward pressure on swap spreads. However, swaps are not only tied to the treasury market. Shorter maturities ranging from 1 to 3 years are tied to the futures markets, and therefore spreads in the shorter maturities will be influenced by the price of the futures strip.

The shape of the yield curve will also have an effect on swap spreads. For example, if the yield curve is flat, then there will be little incentive for any activity in the swap market. In this case, it is likely that the lack of demand will cause spreads to fall.

Terminations and assignments

A very important aspect of liquidity in the swap market is a counterparty's ability to terminate the transaction. In a termination, the counterparties to the swap simply agree on a settlement rate, which is usually the current market rate. The settlement fee paid or received will be the net present value of the annuity reflecting the difference between the swap coupon rate and the settlement rate discounted at the settlement rate. The settlement fee will also reflect net accrued interest and the floating-rate differential unless the swap is terminated on a rollover date.

For example, suppose two counterparties have entered into a £5,000,000 3-year interest rate swap starting on 28 September 1989 and maturing on 28 September 1992. The swap is on a semi-annual actual/365 basis versus 6-month LIBOR, and the swap coupon is 14.10%. After the first year, the cash flows on the swap have been as shown in Table 2.1. By the end of the first year interest rates dropped, and the new swap rate for a 2-year swap is 12.50%. The fixed rate payer decides to terminate the swap effective on the next rollover date, 28 March 1991. The termination value will be the net present value of the cash flows generated by the difference between the old coupon rate, 14.10%, and the new coupon rate, 12.50%, and discounted at the new coupon rate. Therefore, the termination value will be £120,336.35.

Assignments or novations are calculated in the same manner. There is one complicating factor in that this involves the introduction of a third party whose credit standing is crucial to the completion of the assignment. This is especially the case when an institution wishes to assign a whole portfolio. Usually at the outset of a swap transaction, the two counterparties agree that each has the right to assign the contract subject to the other's approval, and this should be written into the documentation.

Decompounding and LIBOR interpolations

Swaps are not necessarily traded with maturities in round years. Firms seeking to offset previous swap positions or to set swaps against

TABLE 2.1   Termination of a swap

Principal: £5 million
Coupon: 14.10% semi-annual vs. 6-month LIBOR
Start date: 28/9/89
Maturity date: 28/9/92

THE CASH FLOWS ON THE SWAP

	FIXED		FLOATING	
ROLLOVER DATE	NUMBER OF DAYS	CASH FLOW	LIBOR FIXING	CASH FLOW
28/3/90	181	349,602.74	15.1250%	375,017.12
28/9/90	184	355,397.26	15.3125%	385,958.90
28/3/91	181	349,602.74		
27/9/91	183	353,465.75		
30/3/92	185	357,328.77		
28/9/92	182	351,534.25		

The termination value will be the NPV of the cash flows generated by the difference between the old coupon rate, 14.10%, and the new coupon rate, 12.50%, discounted at 12.50%.

28/3/91	181	39,671.23
27/9/91	183	40,109.59
30/3/92	185	40,547.95
28/9/92	182	39,890.41
NPV		120,336.35

specific projects will often trade the swap with a maturity known as a 'stump date' or 'cock date'. For instance, a swap may be traded with a maturity in 4 years and 4 months rather than a straight 4-year maturity. The first period, in this example 4 months, is known as the 'stub'. In the US dollar swap market, it is common for the fixed-rate payer to pay a lower coupon rate for the stub, and the lower rate is referred to as the 'decompounded rate'.

For example, suppose a US dollar swap has been traded with a 4 year 4 month maturity at 8.11% on an annual money market basis. The start date of the swap is 25 July 1991, and the maturity date is 25 November 1995. To calculate the decompounded rate, the following equation may be applied:[2]

$$(1 + r/100)\text{no. days}/360 - 1 \times 360/\text{no. days} \times 100$$
$$= \text{decompounded rate.}$$

Thus, in the above example, the decompounded rate would be:

$$(1 + 8.11/100)123/360 - 1 \times 360/123 \times 100 = 7.90\%$$

The fixed-rate payer will make 4 payments at 8.11% and 1 payment at a decompounded rate of 7.90%.

If a swap is being transacted to offset another swap, the start date may not necessarily match the rollover dates. In this event, it is necessary to use a LIBOR interpolation for the first fixing. For example, suppose a swap is transacted with a start date on 18 July 1991 and the first rollover date is 15 October 1991. It will be necessary to interpolate between 2- and 3-month LIBOR for the first fixing. In order to do this, one must calculate the number of days in the 1-month period rolling backwards from the exact date 3 months from the start date, and the number of days in the period from the actual rollover date to 2 months from the start date.

18 September 1991 to 18 October 1991 = 30 days
18 September 1991 to 15 October 1991 = 27 days

2 month LIBOR = 6.03125
3 month LIBOR = 6.0625

Then, the following equation may be applied:

$$[27/30 \times (6.0625 - 6.03125)] + 6.03125 = 6.05938\%$$

Therefore, the interpolated LIBOR fixing will be 6.05938%.

VALUING A SWAP

The aim in valuing a swap is to establish a theoretical price by determining the net present value of the cash flows. The emphasis is on the fixed cash flows rather than the floating cash flows. In many respects it is easy to think of a swap as a bond, except there is no exchange of principal at the beginning and end. The theoretical price of the swap is par if it is trading at its coupon rate.

The internal rate of return (IRR) of the cash flows on the swap represents the net cost of borrowing. For example, if a treasurer raised funds by a 2-year syndicated loan at LIBOR plus a margin and then entered into a swap to change the exposure to fixed, then one could calculate the cash flows from the loan and from the swap, take the IRR of the net cash flows and that would be the net cost of borrowing. What would normally happen would be the floating-rate cash flows from the loan would cancel out the floating payments on the swap (assuming they are equal), leaving the fixed-cash flows as the basis of the IRR.

It is debatable what discount rate one should use to apply to the cash flows. A popular method is to use the current market swap rate, because it is easy to do it this way. However, it is more precise to use the appropriate zero-coupon rates derived from the current swap market yield curve. The reason it is more precise to do it this way is because each cash payment, taken separately, is economically equivalent to a zero-coupon bond, and so it is more accurate to value each cash flow using the zero-coupon rates. The current swap market yield curve should be used to derive the zero-coupon rates, because swap dealers can roughly finance their swap positions at the swap rates. Therefore, it is less accurate to use an alternative curve such as the treasury curve.

Deriving the zero-coupon curve

To derive the zero-coupon swap curve from the par swap curve, each cash flow is discounted by the theoretical spot rate for that period. For example, the following procedures may be used.

Suppose a 1-year swap is trading at 7.00%, and 2-year swap is trading at 7.30%. The cash flow in the first year is 7.30, and the cash flow in the second year is 107.30. If we were to discount the yearly cash flows at 7.30%, the present value of the swap would be 100.00. The aim is to derive the zero-coupon rates which are used as spot discount rates to calculate the present value of each cash flow. The total of the present values of the cash flows at the spot rate should also equal 100.00. To accomplish this, the first period cash flow is discounted at the 1-year swap rate of 7.00%. In this case, $7.30 \times 1/1.07$ equals 6.82. The second period must be discounted at the theoretical spot rate for the period. To solve for this rate, one must first determine what the present value for the period should be. In this example, the present value for the period should be 93.18, representing $100.00 - 6.82$. In other words, the present value of 107.30 in the second year cash flow is 93.18. To solve for the theoretical spot rate, one can follow these steps:

Step 1: $107.30/(1 + i)^2 = 93.18$

Step 2: $93.18 \div 107.30/(1 + i)^2 = 1$

Step 3: $107.30/93.18 = (1 + i)^2$

Step 4: $1.15153 = (1 + i)^2$

Step 5: $1.07310 = 1 + i$

Step 6: $7.31\% = i$

TABLE 2.2 Zero-coupon rates for a 2-year swap

PERIOD	CASH FLOW	DISCOUNT RATE @ 7.30%	PRESENT VALUE	SPOT DISCOUNT	PRESENT VALUE AT SPOT RATE
Year 1 spot discount rate is 7.00%					
Year 2 spot discount rate is 7.31%					
1	7.30	0.93197	6.80	0.93458	6.82
2	107.30	0.86856	93.20	0.86840	93.18
			100.00		100.00

Thus, the cash flows would be as shown in Table 2.2.

We now know that the 1-year zero-coupon rate is 7.00%, and the 2-year zero-coupon rate is 7.31%. To calculate the 3-year zero-coupon rate from the 3-year swap rate which is trading at 7.72%, we must discount the cash flow from year 1, 7.72, at 7.00% which gives us a present value of 7.21. The cash flow from year 2, also 7.72, is discounted at 7.31% which gives us a present value of 6.70. Then, $100.00 - (7.21 + 6.70) = 86.09$. In other words, the present value of 107.72, the cash flow in year 3, is 86.09. Now that we know this, we are in a position to solve for the 3-year zero-coupon rate using the following steps:

Step 1: $107.72/(1 + i)^3 = 86.09$

Step 2: $86.09 \div 107.72/(1 + i)^3 = 1$

Step 3: $107.72/86.09 = (1 + i)^3$

Step 4: $1.25125 = (1 + i)^3$

Step 5: $1.0776 = 1 + i$

Step 6: $7.76\% = i$

Thus, the cash flows would be as shown in Table 2.3.

We know that the zero-coupon rate for year 1 is 7.00%, for year 2 is 7.31% and for year 3 is 7.76%. We are now ready to calculate the zero-coupon rate for year 4, knowing that the 4-year swap rate is 8.02%. The year 1 cash flow, 8.02, is discounted at 7.00%, producing 7.50. The year 2 cash flow, 8.02, is discounted at 7.31%, producing 6.96%. The year 3 cash flow, 8.02, is discounted at 7.76%, producing 6.41. Then, $7.50 + 6.96 + 6.41 = 20.87$, and $100 - 20.87 = 79.13$. Thus, the present value of the cash flow in year 3, 108.02, equals 79.13. We may now solve for the 4-year zero-coupon rate, as follows:

Step 1: $108.02/(1 + i)^4 = 79.13$

TABLE 2.3   Zero-coupon rates for a 3-year swap

PERIOD	CASH FLOW	DISCOUNT RATE @ 7.72%	PRESENT VALUE	SPOT DISCOUNT	PRESENT VALUE AT SPOT RATE
Year 1 spot discount rate is 7.00% Year 2 spot discount rate is 7.31% Year 3 spot discount rate is 7.76%					
1	7.72	0.92833	7.17	0.93458	7.21
2	7.72	0.86180	6.65	0.86840	6.70
3	107.72	0.80004	86.18	0.79915	86.08
			100.00		100.00

Step 2: $79.13 \div 108.02/(1 + i)^4 = 1$

Step 3: $108.02/79.13 = (1 + i)^4$

Step 4: $1.36510 = (1 + i)^4$

Step 5: $1.08091 = 1 + i$

Step 6: $8.091\% = i$

Thus, the cash flows would be as shown in Table 2.4.

Finally, we must find the 5-year zero-coupon rate. We know the 1-year zero-coupon rate is 7.00%, the 2-year zero-coupon rate is 7.31%, the 3-year zero-coupon rate is 7.76%, and the 4-year zero-coupon rate is 8.091%. The 5-year swap rate is 8.28%. The swap cash flow in year 1, 8.28, produces 7.74, the cash flow in year 2, 8.28, produces 7.19, the

TABLE 2.4   Zero-coupon rates for a 4-year swap

PERIOD	CASH FLOW	DISCOUNT RATE @ 8.02%	PRESENT VALUE	SPOT DISCOUNT	PRESENT VALUE AT SPOT RATE
Year 1 spot discount rate is 7.00% Year 2 spot discount rate is 7.31% Year 3 spot discount rate is 7.76% Year 4 spot discount rate is 8.091%					
1	8.02	0.92575	7.42	0.93458	7.50
2	8.02	0.85702	6.87	0.86840	6.96
3	8.02	0.79339	6.36	0.79915	6.41
4	108.02	0.73449	79.34	0.73256	79.13
			100.00		100.00

TABLE 2.5 Zero-coupon rates for a 5-year swap

Year 1 spot discount rate is 7.00%
Year 2 spot discount rate is 7.31%
Year 3 spot discount rate is 7.76%
Year 4 spot discount rate is 8.091%
Year 5 spot discount rate is 8.389%

PERIOD	CASH FLOW	DISCOUNT RATE @ 8.28%	PRESENT VALUE	SPOT DISCOUNT	PRESENT VALUE AT SPOT RATE
1	8.28	0.92353	7.65	0.93458	7.74
2	8.28	0.85291	7.06	0.86840	7.19
3	8.28	0.78769	6.52	0.79915	6.62
4	8.28	0.72746	6.02	0.73256	6.07
5	108.28	0.67183	72.75	0.66846	72.38
			100.00		100.00

cash flow in year 3, 8.28, produces 6.62, and the cash flow in year 4 produces 6.07. Then, 7.74 + 7.19 + 6.62 + 6.07 = 27.62, and 100.00 − 27.62 = 72.38. Thus, the present value of the cash flow in year 5, 108.28, equals 72.38. We may solve for the spot rate using the following steps:

Step 1: $108.28/(1 + i)^5 = 72.38$

Step 2: $72.38 \div 108.28/(1 + i)^5 = 1$

Step 3: $108.28/72.38 = (1 + i)^5$

Step 4: $1.49599 = (1 + i)^5$

Step 5: $1.08389 = 1 + i$

Step 6: $8.389\% = i$

Thus, the cash flows would be as shown in Table 2.5.

The swap trader is now in a position to value the swap by establishing its net present value (see Table 2.6).

RUNNING A PORTFOLIO

How a swap portfolio is used within an institution varies. For example, some financial institutions use a swap portfolio as an outright profit centre while others use the swap portfolio to support the treasury

TABLE 2.6 Valuing a swap from a payer's perspective

5-year swap at 8.28% annual money market
Principal: $10,000,000
Start date: 25/7/91
Maturity date: 25/7/96
First LIBOR setting: 6.4375
Current mid-market rate: 8.25%

Rollover Dates	Number of Days	Fixed Payments	Floating Payments	Current Fixed Market Rate	Current Floating Market Rate	Net Cash Flow	Zero-Coupon Discount Rates	Discounted Cash Flow	Net Present Value
27/1/92	186		332,604.17		332,604.17				−12,191.27
27/7/92	182	846,400	6 mo. LIBOR	843,333.33	6 mo. LIBOR	−3,066.67	7.000	−2,866.05	
25/1/93	182		6 mo. LIBOR		6 mo. LIBOR				
26/7/93	182	837,200	6 mo. LIBOR	834,166.67	6 mo. LIBOR	−3,033.33	7.310	−2,634.14	
25/1/94	183		6 mo. LIBOR		6 mo. LIBOR				
25/7/94	181	837,200	6 mo. LIBOR	834,166.67	6 mo. LIBOR	−3,033.33	7.760	−2,424.08	
25/1/95	184		6 mo. LIBOR		6 mo. LIBOR				
25/7/95	181	839,500	6 mo. LIBOR	836,458.33	6 mo. LIBOR	−3,041.67	8.091	−2,228.20	
25/1/96	184		6 mo. LIBOR		6 mo. LIBOR				
25/7/96	182	841,800	6 mo. LIBOR	838,750.00	6 mo. LIBOR	−3,050.00	8.389	−2,038.80	

department or the corporate finance department. From a strategic point of view, the function of the swap portfolio will determine how the portfolio is actually run.

There are two ways in which the portfolio manager may run the swap book. The first method is to hedge each swap individually as the transaction is taken on to the book. Once the swap is offset, the bond or futures hedge is immediately unwound. Because this approach is slightly inflexible, some portfolio managers aggregate all of the swaps using duration techniques, and then hedge the residual risks. This allows the portfolio manager to tolerate more mismatches. Alternatively, an institution might measure the interest rate and currency exposure and offset this against the assets and liabilities of the institution as a whole.

It is virtually impossible to eliminate all elements of risk. Swap market participants must seek to identify the risks and minimize them where possible through hedging, while trading other risks for profit. If the swap has been hedged with treasuries, a change in the swap spread over treasuries is possible. This is known as spread risk, and it is a risk which cannot be hedged. For example, it was mentioned in the section on swap spreads that an important component of the swap spread is the repo rate. If a swap is being hedged with treasury bonds which are being financed in the repo market, a change in the repo rate will cause a gain or a loss in profitability on the swap and determine the efficiency of a treasury hedge. Nonetheless, the swap market may be viewed as a spread risk market, since the spread is the key tradeable element.

Mismatch risk is one of the most important aspects of swap portfolio risk management. Because the portfolio manager must run the book to suit customer needs and preferences, mismatches may occur in terms of notional principal, maturity date, floating index, floating-rate index reset dates and payment frequencies, payment dates or coupon. Many mismatches can easily be eliminated. For example, a $20 million 5-year swap may be matched with a $10 million 5-year swap, leaving an open position of a $10 million 5-year swap which must be hedged with treasuries. Another example is when a 5-year swap is matched with a 10-year swap, thus leaving open a 5-year swap 5 years forward. This can be hedged in the forward swap market. As a final example, a 5-year swap against 3-month LIBOR may be matched with a 5-year swap against 6-month LIBOR, and the mismatch may be eliminated with a basis swap.

In addition to spread risk, some unhedgeable risks are basis risk, credit risk and reinvestment risk. Basis risk may arise if the swap has been hedged with futures contracts and there is a divergence between LIBOR and the rate implied on the futures contract, thus causing a loss. The swap is exposed to credit risk arising out of the probability that the counterparty will default. The degree of credit risk will vary according to the swap structure. For example, zero-coupon swaps carry more credit risk, because the receiver is entitled to only one payment on maturity. Credit risk will also be slightly increased in cases where there are payment date mismatches, for instance, annual to semi-annual. The semi-annual payer may make a payment only to find that six months later the annual payer defaults. Moreover, the receipt on each rollover date will have to be reinvested, and thus the swap is exposed to reinvestment risk.

HEDGING A SWAP

Hedging has become essential for market-making institutions, because of rapid growth in the market, changing structures of financial institutions, declining revenues and increasing costs. The swap market is a new one, and has grown extensively in a very short period of time. During the growth period in the 1980s, deregulation enabled many institutions to trade products which they were previously prohibited by law to trade. Because of this, the market was forced to cope with many new market entrants, who were competing for trained personnel. This, in combination with the rise in the cost of information systems, led to rising costs and a squeeze on margins. Consequently, it is imperative for traders to protect their profits.

Once the swap has been valued, the trader must choose an appropriate hedge instrument, and determine the price sensitivity of the instrument and the hedge ratio. The payer in a swap buys bonds or futures as a hedge. The risk to the payer is that interest rates go lower; however, if this does happen then the payer will be compensated by an equivalent price rise in the bond or futures bought as a hedge. Conversely, the receiver in the swap sells bonds or futures as a hedge. The risk to the receiver is that interest rates go higher; however, if this happens, then the receiver will be compensated by a decrease in the price of the bonds or futures sold as a hedge. (See Figures 2.2 and 2.3.)

Once the swap trader has valued the swap and determined its price sensitivity, then an appropriate hedging instrument which is highly correlated with the swap must be found. The aim is to select an appropriate hedge whereby any loss on the swap position will be offset by a gain in the security used to hedge the swap. Sterling and US dollar interest rate swaps are priced as a spread over treasuries or futures, so in these markets finding a hedge instrument is little trouble. Fur-

FIGURE 2.2 A payer hedging a swap

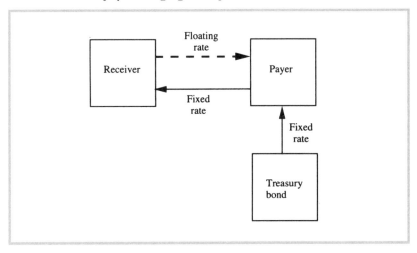

Note: As interest rates go down, the price of the bond will go up.

FIGURE 2.3 A receiver hedging a swap

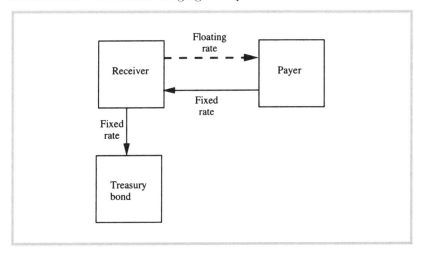

Note: As interest rates go up, the price of the bond will go down.

thermore, these instruments tend to be highly liquid and a repo market exists for financing the hedge position. In less actively traded currencies, this is more likely to be a problem; however, recent developments in the futures markets have reduced this risk substantially.

HEDGING WITH BONDS

Duration

There are three methods which may be used to hedge a swap with bonds: duration, modified duration and present value of a basis point (PVBP). The user of swaps should be aware that the most commonly used method is PVBP, but it is worth understanding the other two concepts as well.

Duration provides a composite measure of interest rate risk assessment, and is an indicator of price sensitivity and volatility. It can be applied to any series of cash flows including annuities, bonds and interest rate swaps. Duration provides us with a reference point to compare two or more instruments. It is also used to establish a hedge ratio for the immunization of a portfolio. The duration of an instrument is the weighted average of the time when payments are made on the instrument and provides a measure of comparative responsiveness of prices to yield changes.

Macaulay (1938) defined duration as:

$$\text{duration} = \sum_{t=1}^{n} \frac{t \cdot (Ct)}{(1 + r)^{t}} \bigg/ P$$

where C = coupon payments in period t; t = time period; n = maturity; r = yield to maturity; and P = price.[3]

In effect the weighted average maturity (duration) is the time periods of payments (t and n) multiplied by the proportion of the bond's value accounted by that payment. Therefore the duration of an instrument is less than or equal to its nominal maturity. If a bond's only cash flow is made to repay both principal and interest on the instrument's maturity date, for instance with a zero-coupon bond, then duration is equal to the nominal maturity period. For instruments with periodic coupons, the average term to maturity (duration) will be less than the instrument's maturity.

Duration is the weighted average length of time between the purchase of an instrument and the receipt of its benefits, where the weightings applied are the present value of the benefits received. For example, if the yield of a bond increases, then the present value of the future cash flows (the price) will decrease. Moreover, the cash flows further in the future will decrease at a greater proportion than those cash flows in the near future. Thus, those cash flows in the distant future will become less important, because the investor will receive a greater proportion of the money in the near future. As a function of this, duration decreases. On the other hand, as yields decrease, then duration will increase because most of the return is received at maturity.

Following on from this concept, usually one can witness lower price sensitivity or duration in an instrument with a higher coupon, a higher yield to maturity, and a shorter term to maturity. Conversely, higher price sensitivity can be witnessed in an instrument with a lower coupon, a lower yield to maturity and a longer term to maturity.

Hedging a swap using duration

In order to establish a hedge ratio, one must calculate the duration of the swap and the duration of the bond being used as the hedge. The hedge ratio is the duration of the swap divided by the duration of the bond.

One might calculate the duration of a 3-year swap and a 3-year note by using the following five steps:

1. List the number of periods in which payments will be made.
2. Calculate the cash flows.
3. Calculate the discount factors for each period to get the net present value of the cash flow.
4. Calculate the price weights of each individual present value cash flow as a proportion of the total net present value.
5. Multiply the number of the period by its corresponding price weight, and add the products together.

It should be noted that the sum of the present values of the individual cash flows is equal to the price of the instrument. It should also be noted that the sum of the price weights should always equal 1. (See Table 2.7)

Using duration, the hedge ratio may be determined by dividing the duration of the swap by the duration of the bond. In this case, the hedge ratio would be:

$$\frac{2.7875}{2.8067} = 0.9932$$

To calculate the number of bonds to be bought or sold, the hedge ratio is then multiplied by the swap principal which would be 10,000,000 × 0.9932 = $9,932,000.

Modified duration

Modified duration is a more commonly used figure as a measure of price volatility. It expresses the price volatility of an instrument for a given change in yield. It is derived as follows:

TABLE 2.7 Calculating the duration of a swap

(a) Duration of the 3-year swap

7.83% coupon
Principal: $10,000,000
Maturing: 5/93
Currently yielding: 7.83%

PERIOD	CASH FLOW	DISCOUNT FACTOR	PRESENT VALUE	PRICE WEIGHT	PRICE WEIGHTED MATURITY
1	7.83	0.9274	7.2614	0.0726	0.0726
2	7.83	0.8600	6.7341	0.0673	0.1346
3	107.83	0.7976	86.0052	0.8601	2.5803
			100.0007	1.0000	2.7875

(b) Duration of the 3-year note

7.00% coupon
Maturing: 5/94
Currently yielding: 7.488%

PERIOD	CASH FLOW	DISCOUNT FACTOR	PRESENT VALUE	PRICE WEIGHT	PRICE WEIGHTED MATURITY
1	7.00	0.9303	6.5124	0.0660	0.0660
2	7.00	0.8655	6.0587	0.0614	0.1227
3	107.00	0.8052	86.1596	0.8727	2.6180
			98.7307	1.0001	2.8067

$$\text{Modified duration} = \text{duration}/1 + \frac{y/f}{100}$$

where y = yield, f = annual coupon frequency.

Therefore, going back to our original example, the modified duration of the 3-year swap can be calculated as follows:

$$\text{Modified duration} = \frac{2.7875}{1 + 7.83/100} = 2.5851$$

In reality, this means that if yields or interest rates in the market move by 1% or 100 basis points, then the price of the 3-year swap will move by approximately 2.5851%. When the calculation is done longhand, we find that a 1% move overnight would represent a change of 2.5397%, which is very close to the estimate using the modified duration calculation.

Following on from the swap calculation, the modified duration of the bond may be calculated as:

$$\frac{2.8067}{1 + 7.488/100} = 2.6112$$

Therefore, the hedge ratio may be determined as:

$$\frac{2.5851}{6.6112} = 0.9900$$

The hedge ratio multiplied by the swap principal is the amount of bonds needed to hedge the swap. In this case it is 10,000,000 × 0.9900 = 9,900,000. Therefore, one would purchase or sell $9,900,000 in treasury bonds to hedge the 3-year swap.

Present value of a basis point

The most common way to determine the hedge ratio for a swap is by using the present value of a basis point (PVBP) method. The objective is to establish what will be the change in the price of the swap and the bond given a change in yield. For example, suppose we wish to hedge a 3-year US$10,000,000 swap with a coupon of 7.83%. The current 3-year note is the 7.00% of 15 May 1994 yielding 7.488%. Table 2.9 shows how the PVBP is established.

It should be noted that the PVBP calculation produced virtually the same volatility as the modified duration calculation. The hedge ratio is determined by the PVBP of the swap divided by the PVBP of the bond multiplied by the principal on the swap. In this case, the trader would hedge the swap with $10,271,000 of the 3-year note. The hedge will exactly offset any movement on the swap as interest rates move. For example, a 10 basis point move would represent an equal gain or loss of $26,500 being 0.0265 × 0.10 × 10,000,000 on the swap and 0.0258 × 0.10 × 10,271,000 on the bond.

TABLE 2.8 Measuring the effectiveness of modified duration

Period	Cash Flow	Discount Factor	Present Value	Period	Cash Flow	Discount Factor	Present Value
1	7.83	0.9274	7.2614	1	7.83	0.9189	7.1947
2	7.83	0.8600	6.7341	2	7.83	0.8443	6.6110
3	107.83	0.7976	86.0052	3	107.83	0.7758	83.6553
			100.0007				97.4610

A 1% move in rates represents a 2.5397% change in price

TABLE 2.9   Present value of a basis point

(a) Of a 3-year swap

Principal: £10,000,000
7.83% coupon
Maturing: 5/94
Currently yielding: 7.83%

	Yield = 7.83%				Yield = 7.84%		
PERIOD	CASH FLOW	DISCOUNT FACTOR	PRESENT VALUE	PERIOD	CASH FLOW	DISCOUNT FACTOR	PRESENT VALUE
1	7.83	0.9274	7.2614	1	7.83	0.9273	7.6208
2	7.83	0.8600	6.7341	2	7.83	0.8599	6.7329
3	107.83	0.7976	86.0052	3	107.83	0.7974	85.9805
			100.0007				99.9742

PVBP = 100.0007 − 99.9742 = 0.0265

(b) Of a 3-year note

7.00% coupon
Maturing: 5/94
Currently yielding: 7.488%

	Yield = 7.488%				Yield = 7.498%		
PERIOD	CASH FLOW	DISCOUNT FACTOR	PRESENT VALUE	PERIOD	CASH FLOW	DISCOUNT FACTOR	PRESENT VALUE
1	7.00	0.9303	6.5124	1	7.00	0.9302	6.5117
2	7.00	0.8655	6.0587	2	7.00	0.8654	6.0576
3	107.00	0.8052	86.1596	3	107.00	0.8050	86.1356
			98.7307				98.7049

PVBP = 98.7307 − 98.7049 = 0.0258

Duration drift and convexity

Interest rate risk appears as a result of assets having a longer duration than the liabilities or planning horizon. The greater the disparity between durations, the greater the risk. The limitations of duration analysis reflect this. The first limitation is known as duration drift. As time passes, a portfolio can be more exposed to rate changes and the duration of the hedge might become too long. Therefore, it is necessary to restructure the portfolio as transactions are matched, as cash is received and as time passes.

Another limitation is convexity. For very small changes in yield, duration analysis is sufficient, because the percentage change in price will be the same for an equal increase or decrease in yield. However, larger changes in the yield curve reduce the accuracy of duration analysis, because prices increase at an increasing rate and decrease at a decreasing rate. The price/yield relationship is curvilinear. The gap between the tangent to the price/yield curve and the curve represents the error due to convexity.

As interest rates change, duration-matched portfolios can diverge. For example, two bonds may have the same yield and duration, but they may respond differently to large changes in interest rates. A greater curvature of a price/yield curve will denote a superior perform-ance in a bond. Thus, all other things equal, one should seek to buy the bond with the highest convexity. Positive convexity implies that as the yield increases, the duration decreases. Negative convexity implies that as the yield decreases, the duration increases. Convexity can be used in establishing a hedge ratio insofar as a long position should have a greater convexity than the short position.

As a rule of thumb, one might take note of the following points:[4]

- For bonds with equal duration, zero-coupon bonds have the least convexity and high-coupon bonds have the most convexity.
- For bonds with equal maturities, zero-coupon bonds have the most convexity.
- Increasing duration by an amount that is more than one increases convexity by more than that amount.
- As yields decrease, duration increases.
- As yields increase, duration decreases.

HEDGING WITH FUTURES

Swaps against futures strips

A futures strip is a stream or series of short-term futures contracts, for example, Eurodollar futures or short sterling futures, which when grossed up will generate a return for a term equal to the length of the strip. The strip can be used to hedge maturing in up to 10 years depending on the number of futures contracts quoted. As in the case with hedging with treasury bonds, the payer in the swap will buy futures and the receiver of the swap will sell futures. Furthermore, in pricing the swaps, market-makers will use the strip as a benchmark and will often seek to pay a given amount of basis points under the strip and receive at a given amount of basis points over the strip.

A 1-year futures strip may be calculated in two steps. The first step is to establish the amount of compound interest that would be earned from placing $1,000,000 on deposit for each period at the implied futures rate. The second step is to apply the following equation:[5]

$$\text{Strip} = (\text{total interest accrued} \times 360)$$
$$\div (1,000,000 \times \text{total number of days})$$

For example, let us suppose today is 17 July, and the Eurodollar futures prices are quoted as follows:

Contract month	Price	Implied interest rate	No of days in the period
September 91	93.70	6.30	63 days
December 91	93.12	6.88	91 days
March 92	93.04	6.96	91 days
June 92	92.65	7.35	91 days
September 92	92.30	7.70	30 days

The compound interest would be calculated as:

Period	Principal	Futures interest rate	Days	Interest
1	1,000,000.00	6.30	63	11,025.00
2	1,011,025.00	6.88	91	17,582.85
3	1,028,607.85	6.96	91	18,096.64
4	1,046,704.49	7.35	91	19,446.90
5	1,066,151.39	7.70	30	6,841.14
Total				72,992.53

Thus, the 1-year strip can be calculated as:

$$\frac{72,992.53 \times 360}{366,000,000}$$

$$= \frac{26,277,310.80}{366,000,000} = 7.18\%$$

The swap may be quoted in the market as 7.16 − 7.26.

If one wanted to calculate the strip with a start date and rollover dates exactly matching the futures cycle beginning with the expiry date of the September futures contract (18 September) the following equation may be employed:

$$[(R1 + R2 + R3 + R4) \div 1600 + 1]^4 \times 100 - 100$$

Using the implied futures rates as above, the strip would be:

$$[(6.88 + 6.96 + 7.35 + 7.70) \div 1600 + 1]^4 \times 100 - 100 = 7.42\%$$

A payer in a 1-year swap would buy a 1-year strip of futures which would generate a yield of 7.18% in the first example and 7.42% in the second example. Likewise, a receiver in a 1-year swap would sell the strip.

Now, let us assume a $10 million 1-year swap has been traded, and we have paid 7.16%. How many futures contracts must be bought to hedge the swap? As above, one must first calculate the compound interest which will be earned on $10 million using the implied futures rate from each period as the interest rate.

PERIOD	PRINCIPAL	FUTURES INTEREST RATE	DAYS	PRINCIPAL PLUS INTEREST
1	10,000,000	6.30	63	10,110,250
2	10,110,250	6.88	91	10,286,078
3	10,286,078	6.96	91	10,467,044
4	10,467,044	7.35	91	10,661,513
5	10,661,513	7.70	30	10,729,924

The hedge ratio may be determined by dividing the value per basis point of each period's principal plus interest by $25, which is the value per basis point per Eurodollar futures contract.

Period
1 $(10,000,000 \times 0.0001 \times 63/360) \div 25 = 7$ Sept. 91 contracts
2 $(10,110,250 \times 0.0001 \times 91/360) \div 25 = 10$ Dec. 91 contracts
3 $(10,286,078 \times 0.0001 \times 91/360) \div 25 = 10$ March 92 contracts
4 $(10,467,044 \times 0.0001 \times 91/360) \div 25 = 11$ June 92 contracts
5 $(10,661,513 \times 0.0001 \times 30/360) \div 25 = 4$ Sept. 92 contracts

One may test the effectiveness of the hedge by proposing the scenario that the market has moved adversely to the swap position, and swap rates have dropped by 10 basis points a few weeks after entering into the transaction. For this example, assume that the implied futures rates have dropped by 10 basis points as well.

Period
1   7 contracts × (93.80 − 93.70) × $2,500 = 1,750
2   10 contracts × (93.22 − 93.12) × $2,500 = 2,500
3   10 contracts × (93.14 − 93.04) × $2,500 = 2,500
4   11 contracts × (93.75 − 92.65) × $2,500 = 2,750
5   4 contracts × (92.40 − 92.30) × $2,500 = 1,000

A 10 basis point loss on the swap would represent $10,000 being $10 million times 0.0010. However, this loss would be offset by a profit on the futures hedge of $10,500. The slight overperformance of the hedge in this example may be attributed to the fact that futures contracts are for standard sizes which may not exactly match the principal amount to be hedged. A slight overperformance is beneficial, as the profit will cover brokerage on the futures contracts. One must beware of larger movements in rates which may cause a greater overperformance or underperformance of the hedge. The example below shows the effect of a 50 basis point move.

Period
1   7 contracts × (94.20 − 93.70) × $2,500 = 8,750
2   10 contracts × (93.62 − 93.12) × $2,500 = 12,500
3   10 contracts × (93.54 − 93.04) × $2,500 = 12,500
4   11 contracts × (93.15 − 92.65) × $2,500 = 13,750
5   4 contracts × (92.80 − 92.30) × $2,500 = 5,000

A 50 basis point loss on the swap would represent $50,000 being $10 million times 0.0050. However, this loss would be offset by a profit on the futures hedge of $52,500, showing an overperformance of $2,500 on the hedge. It is for this reason that hedge monitoring is essential, so that adjustments can be made in accordance with interest rate movements.

THE CHICAGO MERCANTILE EXCHANGE SWAPS COLLATERAL DEPOSITORY

The Chicago Mercantile Exchange (CME) has asked investment and commercial banks to join a swaps collateral depository to be known as the CME Depository Trust Co. (DTC). The scheme aims to minimize risk and maximize efficiency in the derivatives market by automating and simplifying a highly labour-intensive process. The CME DTC is a joint effort of the CME, SunGard Capital Markets, Inc. and the Society for Worldwide Interbank Financial Telecommunication (SWIFT).

Once it is operational, the Depository will receive and accept swaps transactions from commercial and investment banks, mark them to market, and report positions on collateral held for member banks. It will be able to evaluate and collateralize existing swaps transactions as well as new swaps positions, enabling firms to more efficiently manage their entire book of swaps.

Swaps dealers now deposit collateral with each of their trading partners on a bilateral basis. The CME Depository will be a central place for all of a dealer's collateral information related to swaps transactions. This way, a dealer can pool its debits and credits on a daily basis to meet its collateral needs. See Appendix 1 for more information on the CME Depository Trust Co.

SUMMARY

A 'generic' or 'plain vanilla' interest rate swap involves an agreement between parties to exchange periodic payments calculated on the basis of a specified coupon rate and a mutually agreed notional principal amount. It involves the exchange of floating-rate interest obligations for fixed-rate interest obligations. The fixed-rate payer is known as the payer in the swap, and the floating-rate payer is known as the receiver in the swap. In most currencies, the fixed-rate component is normally calculated as a spread over treasuries, and the floating-rate component is LIBOR.

Swaps are usually transacted over the telephone. The two counterparties must agree the fixed rate, the floating rate for the first period and floating-rate basis, the day basis, the start date and maturity date, the rollover dates, the governing law and documentation prior to closing the deal. The transaction is followed by a fax or telex confirmation, and later, a written confirmation and documents must be signed to formalize the agreement.

There are several factors which affect swap pricing. Typically, they are the benchmark price, supply and demand factors, transaction costs and credit risk. In turn, swap spreads are affected by the cost of carry of the hedge instrument, supply and demand, credit arbitrage and the shape of the yield curve.

Swaps are a flexible management tool in that they can be terminated or assigned to another counterparty if the swap is no longer needed by the user. They must be monitored and periodically valued, preferably using the zero-coupon swap curve. Depending on the currency, they can easily be hedged using treasury bonds or futures. A payer in the swap will hedge by buying treasuries or futures, and a receiver in the swap will hedge by selling treasuries or futures. The US dollar and sterling swap markets closely track the treasury markets, thus providing a highly correlated hedge instrument. Short-term interest rate futures contracts in most major currencies may be used to calculate strips (as long as 10 years in the case of Eurodollars), which provide a highly correlated hedge instrument for swaps, especially those with shorter maturities.

Notes

1. A/360 means 'the actual number of days/360' and A/365 means 'the actual number of days/365'.

2. It should be noted that if the swap is traded on a bond basis, then 365 should be substituted for 360.

3. The basic assumptions of Macaulay's (and other later) assessments of duration assume a flat yield curve, nominal yield rates rather than forward rates, and permit only single parallel changes in the yield curve.

4. See *Concepts and Applications: Understanding Duration and Convexity*. Chicago Board of Trade, 1990, p. 10.

5. 365 days should be substituted for 360 when calculating a short sterling strip.

Bibliography

Antl, Boris (ed.) (1986). *Swap Finance, Vols I and II*. London: Euromoney Publications Ltd.

Concepts and Applications: Understanding Duration and Convexity (1990). Chicago Board of Trade.

Das, Satyajit (1989). *Swap Financing*. London: IFR Publishing Ltd.

Dawaller, Ira G. (1989). 'Interest rate swaps versus Eurodollar strips', *Financial Analysis Journal*, vol. 45, September/October, pp. 55–61.

DeCovny, Sherree and Tacchi, Christine (1991). *Hedging Strategies*. Cambridge: Woodhead-Faulkner (Publishers) Ltd.

Durr, Barbara (1991). 'Chicago looks to a new future', *Financial Times*, 21 June, p. 27.

Fabozzi, Frank J. and Pollack, Irving M. (1983). *The Handbook of Fixed Income Securities*. Homewood, Ill: Dow Jones–Irwin.

Hamilton, James (1990). 'An introduction to swap products', *The Treasurer*, vol. 12, no. 2, February, pp. 6–9.

Henderson, Schuyler K. and Price, John A. M. (1988). *Currency and Interest Rate Swaps*, 2nd edition. London: Butterworths.

Macaulay, F. R. (1938). 'Some theoretical problems suggested by the movement of interest rates, bond yields, and stock prices in the US since 1856', National Bureau of Economic Research, New York.

Rosen, Lawrence R. (1986). *Investing in Zero Coupon Bonds*. New York: John Wiley & Sons.

Smith, Donald J. (1988). 'Measuring the gains from arbitraging the swap market', *Financial Executive*, vol. 4, March/April, pp. 46–9.

CURRENCY SWAPS | 3

The currency swap developed from the parallel loan and was the forerunner to the interest rate swap. At present, currency swaps are less actively traded than interest rate swaps, but nonetheless, currency swaps make up a significant proportion of the overall swap market. Rather than a trading instrument in its own right, the currency swap may be used by treasurers and fund managers as a flexible asset and liability management tool.

DESCRIPTION OF CROSS-CURRENCY SWAPS

A currency swap is a contract to exchange interest payments in one currency for those denominated in another currency. The currency swap functions virtually the same as a parallel or back-to-back loan. Although the currency swap market is older than the interest rate swap market it is smaller and less sophisticated.

In the early to mid-1980s currency swaps became popular for three main reasons. First, central bank regulations forced banks to fund term floating-rate assets with term liabilities as opposed to short-term deposits. Second, counterparties sought to take advantage of one another's borrowing capacity in the various international markets. Finally, a lower cost of funds motivated counterparties to accept credit risk in the swap.

Now, there are several reasons why firms use currency swaps. First, the currency swap may be used to hedge against foreign exchange risk. A firm may transform the currency denomination of its borrowings to lock in unrealized gains on foreign currency liabilities at a time when exchange rates are favourable. Second, a lower cost of funding may be obtained by borrowing in a foreign country and swapping back to the domestic currency. Third, a firm may be able to use their surplus funds more effectively in blocked currencies. Fourth, the use of swaps may be a way of circumventing exchange control regulations. Fifth, currency swaps may be used as a means of exploiting arbitrage opportunities. Finally, the currency swap may be used in conjunction with a portfolio of assets providing a vehicle for more active portfolio management.

Swaps originate from two areas: the foreign exchange markets and the capital markets, and the term often causes confusion. In the foreign exchange markets a currency swap is a spot sale and forward purchase of one currency for another. The concept of the currency swap in the capital markets sense goes one step further. Just as an interest rate swap can be thought of as a series of forward-forward contracts, a currency swap is very much like a series of long-term foreign exchange contracts. Also, a long-term foreign exchange contract may be thought of as a fixed-to-fixed zero-coupon currency swap. Currency swaps may be used in the absence of a forward foreign exchange market for medium- to long-term maturities between two currencies.

In the capital markets a currency swap usually involves a stream of interest payments in conjunction with a foreign exchange transaction. Capital market based currency swaps are usually fixed/floating, with the floating side being US dollars. However, currency swaps may be transacted on a fixed-fixed or floating-floating basis.

A currency swap usually entails an initial exchange of currencies and a reverse exchange on maturity; however, it is not mandatory to exchange principal particularly if the swap is against existing borrowings. Interest payments are made by one counterparty to another based on the principal in the currency being held. A bank may stand between two counterparties either for credit reasons or because the needs of the counterparties do not exactly match.

The exchange rate agreed will normally be based on the spot rate; however, it is possible to do the exchange with off-market spot rates, but this would be reflected in the coupon on the swap. Both parties know what their future liabilities are, but as the spot rate at maturity is likely to differ from the spot rate at start, one party to the swap will make a foreign exchange profit and the other party a loss. One way of resolving this problem is to do a front-to-back exchange where the exchange rate used at the start of the swap is the same as the exchange rate used at maturity.

The rate agreed on the swap will depend on the general expectations of future currency movements, including potential devaluation, and the influence those expectations have over supply and demand for swaps in that currency in the market. When demand is one-sided, the rate may not be favourable. Pricing tends to be subject to negotiation, but the basis for price will reflect the interest rate differentials between the currencies involved in relation to the government bonds for the particular maturity. Governmental policy and credit rating will also affect the price.

Many banks now act as active dealers in currency swaps. However, very large transactions may involve a number of counterparties as no one trader is prepared to take that degree of risk on their books. Moreover, since the late 1980s, new capital adequacy requirements have made currency swaps prohibitively expensive for many banks. Capital adequacy is discussed in Chapter 6.

Currency swaps have played an important role in the Eurobond markets, enabling large borrowers to borrow at sub-LIBOR rates. Good quality names are able to borrow in certain currencies at very low rates. The Australian dollar and New Zealand dollar markets have been notable, particularly in the 1980s. Borrowings in these currencies are then swapped into a currency actually required by the borrower producing cheaper funding than direct borrowing in that currency. The cheap rates are often due to the fact that the small investor in an obscure market is more willing to invest in an internationally renowned name, such as the World Bank, and will accept a lower return than some professional investors. Some markets also have a smaller yield differential between grades of borrowers.

VARIOUS FORMS OF CURRENCY SWAPS

Cross-currency fixed-to-fixed swap

The motivation for this type of swap is that each of the two counter-parties have access to cheap funds in different countries. Each counterparty can raise funds in the country in which they have advantage and enter into a swap whereby the payments are transformed into the currency that they prefer.

For example (see Figure 3.1), Company A is an American company and is thus US dollar based. Company A's problem is that it has issued bonds in the domestic market on a few occasions. Consequently, it can no longer issue bonds at a cheap rate, because the demand has been saturated. On the other hand, Company A has not been a frequent borrower in Switzerland and is considered a good credit there. Thus, if A raises funds in a Swiss franc issue, it will be able to borrow at a lower rate. This is because Company A is considered a good credit from a

FIGURE 3.1 A cross-currency fixed-to-fixed swap

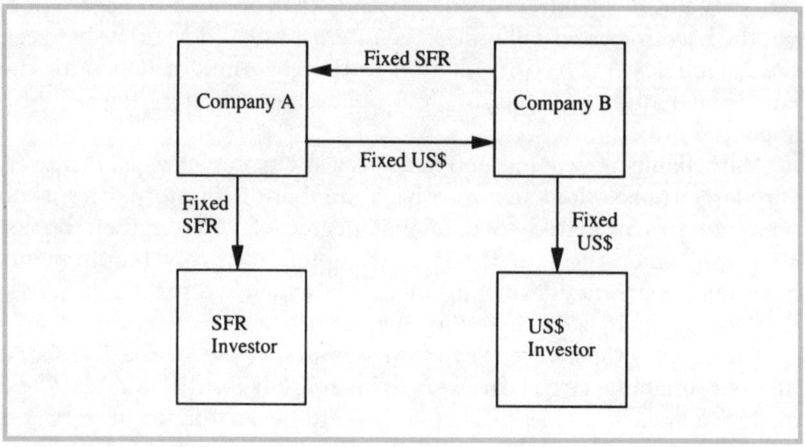

safe domicile, that is, the United States, so Swiss investors will have a demand for Company A's bonds.

Company B is in the opposite position and can raise cheap funds by issuing a bond in US dollars. Company A can be matched with Company B in a currency swap. Company A will service the borrowing cost of Company B, and Company B will service the borrowing cost of Company A.

This may involve an exchange of principal by way of a front-to-back exchange. At the start of the swap, Company A sells Swiss francs and buys US dollars. Company B buys Swiss francs and sells US dollars. During the swap, Company A pays interest denominated in US dollars to Company B, thus servicing the interest payments on the dollar issue. Company B pays interest denominated in Swiss francs to Company A to service the interest payments on the Swiss franc issue. At the maturity of the swap, Company A buys Swiss francs and sells US dollars, and Company B sells Swiss francs and buys US dollars. This end transaction enables the two counterparties to redeem their respective issues.

Example Company A has raised funds in sterling for 3 years at 12.00%. Company B has an outstanding 3-year US dollar issue with a coupon of 9.50%. Company B is prepared to swap out of its dollar debt into a sterling obligation at a cost of 12.50%. The exchange rate is $1.6530 = £1. Company A's borrowing cost in sterling is as follows:

Proceeds:	100.00
Fees:	2.25%
Net proceeds:	97.75

Thus, Company A's net proceeds are £97,750,000.

The present value of Company A's future principal and interest obligation is discounted at Company B's target rate of 12.50% as follows:

CASH FLOW	DISCOUNT RATE	PRESENT VALUE
12	$1/1.1250$	10.67
12	$1/(1.1250)^2$	9.48
112	$1/(1.1250)^3$	78.66
		98.81

Thus, the present value is £98,810,000. This figure is then converted into US $163,332,930, being £98,810,000 × 1.6530. The dollar equivalent of the present value of Company A's principal and interest obligation is multiplied by the rate Company B is paying on its current debt obligation to give the annual payment:

Nominal	$163,332,930
Interest	× 9.50%
Annual payment	$15,516,628

Company A's net proceeds from the sterling issue are sold for US dollars:

$$£97,750,000 \times 1.6530 = \$161,580,750.$$

The two swap counterparties will enter into an exchange of principal (see Figure 3.2) whereby Company A will pay Company B £97,750,000 and Company B will pay Company A US $161,580,750.

To find the all-in cost of simulating fixed-rate US dollar debt, first the net proceeds in dollars must be divided by the present value of the principal plus interest payments in US dollars. Thus, 161,580,750 ÷ 163,332,930 = 0.9893. Second, one must calculate the yield-to-maturity on a 3-year note with a present value of 98.93 and a coupon of 9.50%. The yield-to-maturity is 9.93% as follows:

CASH FLOW	DISCOUNT RATE	PRESENT VALUE
9.50	$1/1.0993$	8.64
9.50	$1/(1.0993)^2$	7.86
109.50	$1/(1.0993)^3$	82.43
		98.93

FIGURE 3.2 Fixed-to-fixed swap: exchange of principal

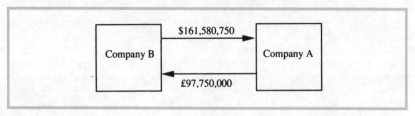

Therefore, during the swap, Company A will pay to Company B 9.93% on US $161,580,750 and Company B will pay to Company A 12.00% on £97,750,000 (see Figure 3.3).

At maturity, the two counterparties will re-exchange principal amounts. Company A will pay to Company B $161,580,750 and Company B will pay to Company A £97,750,000 (see Figure 3.4).

Cross-currency floating-to-fixed swap

Often a non-US dollar based bank has medium-term floating assets denominated in dollars. The bank needs to fund its medium-term floating dollar assets with medium-term floating dollar liabilities. However, it can raise funds cheaply only on a fixed-rate basis in its domestic currency. A swap is a way to solve this problem (see Figure 3.5). For example, Counterparty A is domiciled in the United States,

FIGURE 3.3 Fixed-to-fixed swap: during the swap

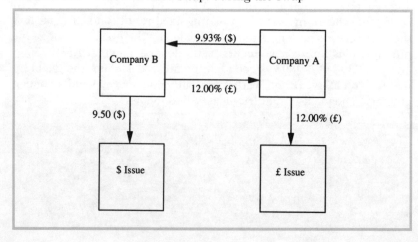

FIGURE 3.4 Fixed-to-fixed swap: re-exchange of principal

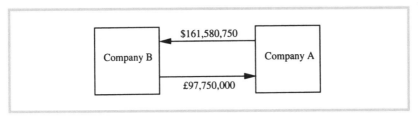

and Counterparty B is domiciled in Switzerland. In this case, Counterparty A is in a position to borrow cheaply in US dollars on a floating-rate basis and Counterparty B is in a position to borrow cheaply on a fixed-rate basis in Swiss francs. Each counterparty can use their comparatively strong borrowing capacity to reduce the overall cost of funds by entering into a currency swap.

Counterparty A can borrow floating-rate funds in the US dollar money market at LIBOR plus a margin. Counterparty B can borrow fixed-rate funds cheaply in Swiss francs by way of a bond issue. During the swap, Counterparty B can pay floating-rate dollars to Counterparty A to service the dollar loan. Counterparty A can pay fixed-rate Swiss francs to Counterparty B to service the Swiss franc loan.

Example Suppose a US company launches a 5-year issue to raise DM 100 million. The coupon rate is 10.00% and the current foreign exchange rate is DM 1.7860 = US$1.

FIGURE 3.5 Cross-currency floating-to-fixed

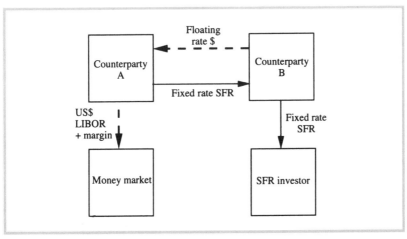

Bond issue:
Issuer   US company
Amount   DM 100 million
Term   5 years
Coupon   10.00%
Issue price   101.25
Fees   2.00%
Expenses   0.25% per annum or DM 250,000
Payment   4 weeks from the launch

Swap:
Type   DM fixed vs. US$ floating
Structure   US company receives fixed DM and pays
                   floating US$
Coupon rate   10.00%
All-in swap quote 10.60/10.80 annual

The swap counterparty reimburses the issue fees up to par to the US company to provide it with proceeds of DM 100 million. At commencement, assuming a spot exchange rate of DM 1.7860 = US$1, the US company will pay over the issue proceeds of DM 99 million to the swap counterparty. The DM 99 million is determined as follows:

$$101.25\% - 2\% = 99.25\%$$
$$100 \text{ million} \times 99.25\% = 99,250,000$$
$$99,250,000 - 250,000 = 99,000,000$$

In turn, the US company will receive US$55,431,131, being DM 99,000,000 ÷ 1.7860 (see Figure 3.6).

Over the life of the swap, the US company receives and the counterparty pays 10.00% on DM 99,000,000. The US company pays, and the counterparty receives 6-month US$ LIBOR minus a spread on $55,431,131.

In order to determine the spread under LIBOR that the US counterparty will pay, the pricing of the swap will have to be adjusted

FIGURE 3.6 Floating-to-fixed swap: exchange of principal

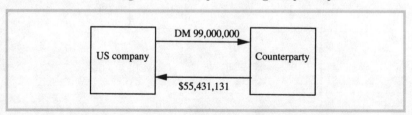

to account for fee amortization and for the delayed start to give an all-in swap payment as follows:

Annual swap rate	10.60
Fee amortization	0.26
Delayed start	0.04
All-in swap payment	10.90

Because the all-in swap payment is 10.90% and the coupon on the swap is 10.00%, the US counterparty will pay US$ LIBOR minus 90 basis points on the floating side of the swap (see Figure 3.7).

At maturity, the US company receives DM 99,000,000 to repay the bondholders and the US company pays $55,431,131 back to the counterparty (see Figure 3.8).

Cross-currency floating-floating (basis) swap

This final type of currency swap is used as an alternative to the foreign exchange market. It does not tend to be widely used because of capital adequacy requirements, but it is certainly worth knowing how to use it. Its main advantage is that the counterparties can obtain a term commitment which would roll over an effective forward foreign exchange contract according to an agreed period.

An example would be for a German counterparty and a US counterparty to enter into a 6-month LIBOR basis swap whereby the German counterparty is able to change a Deutschemark liability into a

FIGURE 3.7 Floating-to-fixed swap: during the swap

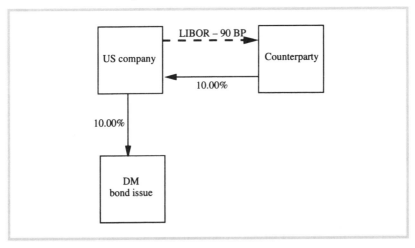

FIGURE 3.8 Floating-to-fixed swap: re-exchange of principal

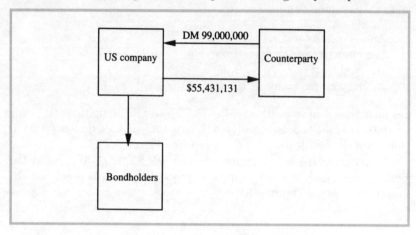

FIGURE 3.9 Cross-currency basis swap

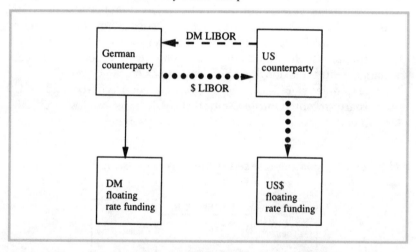

dollar liability, while the US counterparty is able to change a dollar liability into a Deutschemark liability (see Figure 3.9).

HEDGING CURRENCY SWAPS

Hedging cross-currency interest rate risk can be an expensive and difficult manoeuvre due to lack of liquidity or the inefficiency of a particular market. Of course, the degree of difficulty will vary from currency to currency. In order to hedge a currency swap, the swap trader must look at the swap from a cash market view point. In other words, if one is a receiver of fixed Australian dollars and a payer of floating US dollars, one is effectively long an Australian dollar bond and short a US dollar floating-rate note. As a hedge, the swap trader would sell an Australian dollar bond and invest the proceeds by buying a US dollar floating-rate note. Alternatively, if one is a payer of fixed Australian dollars and a receiver of floating US dollars, then one is effectively short an Australian dollar bond and long a US dollar floating-rate note. In this case, the appropriate hedge would be to buy an Australian dollar bond and fund the position by selling a US dollar floating-rate note or by borrowing on an overnight basis.

The impact of the euro[1]

With European Monetary Union (EMU) coming into effect in January 1999, banking authorities are developing solutions to many of the issues relating to the transition to the new European currency, the euro. Among the financial industry groups and trade associations providing input into the preparation are the European Commission, the European Monetary Institute, the Bank of England and other national banks, and tax authorities.

The International Swaps and Derivatives Association (ISDA) is coordinating the preparation of those involved with swaps and other Over-the-Counter (OTC) derivatives for EMU. ISDA maintains four separate task forces dealing with different aspects of the process: market practice; documentation; legal/regulatory; and tax, accounting and capital. The organization is also educating its international membership. For example, ISDA is involved in establishing price sources for the euro.

Meanwhile, the financial world must prepare for EMU to have an impact on every aspect of the business, ranging from software programs to the technicalities of contracts written in different currencies which will eventually disappear. Swaps agreements are often dealt under New York law, and New York State has already adopted legislation stating that the euro is an acceptable commercial substitute.

Of major concern is the redenomination of the open swap contracts, as well as instruments used to hedge swaps. In the UK, for example, it has been recommended that gilt prices should be quoted as decimals rather than fractions, and the day-count convention (A/365) should be retained unless there is a wider initiative for harmonization in Europe. During the transition period, Bankers Automated Clearing Services (BACS) and the Cheque and Credit Clearing Co. intend to ensure that payments can be made in euro and credited to sterling accounts.

Several contracts on the London International Financial Futures and Options Exchange (LIFFE) used to hedge swaps – such as the three-month Euromark, Short Sterling, Eurolira, and three-month ECU – will be effected by the change. In March 1996, LIFFE made legal provisions for its money-market contracts so that they will settle against the British Bankers Association (BBA) euro LIBOR interest rates, if, and as long as:

● the euro is the lawful currency of the relevant country
● there is a fixed exchange rate between the national currency and the euro
● the start of EMU does not fall within 20 business days prior to the last trading day of the relevant delivery month.

LIFFE included provisions to reflect any change in market conventions. The BBA has indicated that it will publish a euro rate and is determining the basis for its calculation.

LIFFE listed the March 1999 delivery month for its three-month ECU contract on 18 March 1997. Subject to EMU going ahead as anticipated, this contract will be denominated in euro with a simple 1:1 conversion rate. The first-ever euro futures contract now trades on LIFFE, and has a contract size of euro 1,000,000 and a tick value of euro 25.

LIFFE has also completed a number of initiatives to ensure a smooth transition to the euro. These include:

● launch of the one-month Euromark future
● introduction of four additional quarterly deliveries and serial months for the three-month Euromark future
● listing of extra delivery/expiry months for the Eurolira future and option

The ultimate effect of EMU on outstanding contracts executed prior to 1999 has yet to be determined. Swaps market participants want to ensure continuity of contract, and avoid terminating the swap on the basis of *force majeure*. Short-term transactions are less complex than longer-dated contracts, because there is less certainty over time.

SUMMARY

The currency swap market, which evolved out of the parallel loan concept, was given a boost by the need for banks to circumvent central bank regulations and the need for banks and corporate users to reduce funding costs. In addition to these applications, the currency swap is now an effective tool for managing long-term foreign exchange risk and interest rate risk.

A currency swap may be dealt using one of three structures: fixed-to-fixed, floating-to-fixed or floating-to-floating. Most currency swaps are done in conjunction with debt issues. They are seldom used as a trading instrument, because they are more difficult to hedge than interest rate swaps, and capital adequacy requirements make them expensive. Unlike the interest rate swap, the currency swap will usually involve an exchange of principal on the start date and a re-exchange of principal on the maturity date. The principal amounts in the relevant currencies are usually exchanged at the prevailing spot rate, and the same exchange rate is used in the initial exchange and the re-exchange.

Note

1. See *Practical Issues Arising from the Introduction of the Euro*, pp. 52–60.

Bibliography

Antl, Boris (ed.) (1986). *Swap Finance, Vols I and II*. London: Euromoney Publications Ltd.

Das, Satyajit (1989). *Swap Financing*. London: IFR Publishing Ltd.

DeCovny, Sherree and Tacchi, Christine (1991). *Hedging Strategies*. Cambridge: Woodhead-Faulkner (Publishers) Ltd.

Hamilton, James (1990). 'An introduction to swap products', *The Treasurer*, vol. 12, no. 2, February, pp. 6–9.

Henderson, Schuyler K. and Price, John A. M. (1988). *Currency and Interest Rate Swaps*, 2nd edition. London: Butterworths.

Practical Issues Arising from the Introduction of the Euro, Issue No. 4, 24 April 1997, London: The Bank of England.

Tiner, John and Conneely, Joe. 'Taking swaps into account', *The Treasurer*, vol. 12, no. 2, February, pp. 30–4.

SWAPS AND THE EUROBOND MARKET

4

The Eurobond market provides a means for companies to raise funds, often at preferential rates, and extend their investor base. At the same time the investor is able to purchase securities issued by foreign companies while still preserving anonymity. Combined with a swap, the Eurobond provides additional flexibility in asset and liability management to both the borrower and the investor. Thus, over recent years, the Eurobond market has lain at the heart of the swaps market.

THE GROWTH OF THE INTERNATIONAL DEBT MARKET

Prior to the relaxation of financial market regulations, firms which were considered weaker credits were forced to borrow funds from commercial banks, finance companies or insurance companies at unattractive rates. After the introduction of SEC rule number 415, it became cheaper and easier for large companies to bring a public debt issue to the market. Moreover, tax regulations increased the occurrence of certain types of issues such as zero-coupon bonds.[1] Overall cheaper costs of issuing gave a boost to the US domestic debt market, not only for companies issuing investment grade securities, but also those issuing bonds rated below investment grade or 'junk bonds'. By accessing the public market, the weaker credit firm was able to enjoy similar privileges to the companies with stronger credit ratings. The junk bond market grew rapidly, and by the end of 1988 was worth more than $180 billion and represented more than 20% of the corporate bond market.[2]

While investors were prepared to buy investment grade debt issues, there was no protection from eroded returns in periods of high inflation. On the other hand, junk bonds were often more attractive, not only because of their high yields, but also because their higher default risk promoted a greater link between the bond value and the issuer's asset values. As a result, junk bonds proved to be less interest rate sensitive than investment grade bonds, thus giving rise to their popularity.

The supply side for debt instruments in the 1980s was dominated by a wave of corporate restructuring, often by takeover, divestment or recapitalization. Organic growth as well as growth in the form of mergers and acquisitions was largely financed by public debt issues easily sold to investors to quench their thirst for high returns. However, restructuring often had an effect on the firm's credit standing which translated into 'event risk'. As a result, the demand side was affected. When purchasing debt instruments, investors came to demand new enticements in order to accept this risk. This gave rise to the market for floating-rate notes, zero-coupon bonds and putable bonds.

Furthermore, the growth of technology and the improvement in communications have contributed to the growth of the bond as well as other markets. Easy access to information about companies and specific debt issues has turned the market into a global one.

THE EUROBOND MARKET

The first Eurobond issue was in 1957, but the real growth in the market began in the 1970s. At that time, US corporations were subject to extremely strict registration and disclosure regulations regarding debt issues in the domestic market. In addition, the government imposed a 30% withholding tax on interest paid to foreign holders of domestic issues. By accessing the Eurobond market, the issuer was able to circumvent the domestic regulations, expand its investor base and sometimes raise funds more cheaply than in the domestic market. The investor gained by having access to securities issued by a wider range of corporate names, and by being able to buy securities issued by US corporations in bearer form, thus preserving anonymity. Consequently, the Eurobond market experienced rapid growth from a total annual issue of $2.1 billion in 1974 to $24 billion in 1980.[3]

Nowadays, there are several different categories of Eurobond issuers including supranational institutions, governments, governmental agencies such as utilities and nationalized industries, provinces and states, corporations and banks. The market is receptive to the best quality borrowers and issues ranging between 3 and 10 years. Borrowers raise funds in various currencies including US dollars, Deutschemarks, Japanese yen, ECU, sterling, French francs, Dutch guilders, Australian dollars, New Zealand dollars, Italian lira and Spanish pesetas. A vast number of Eurobond issues are swap driven. By 1987, 70% of all new debt issues in the Eurobond market were swapped.

Regulation of the Eurobond market

There is no one body which has ultimate authority over the primary Eurobond market; however, most underwriters are stock exchange members, and bonds are generally listed on the London or Luxemburg stock exchange. Thus, the underwriters' activities, including the preparation of the prospectus, are conducted in accordance with stock exchange rules.

Another organization affects the regulation of the Eurobond market. The Association of International Bond Dealers (AIBD) makes regulations and recommendations, but it doesn't have any legal power. The AIBD makes rules and regulations regarding the execution of client orders, settlement instructions, confirmation of accrued interest and delivery requirements. The AIBD also performs the function of arbitrator in situations where a seller is unable to make delivery of the securities or a buyer is unable to pay for the securities purchased.

The issue of a Eurobond must comply with the laws of the country in which the bond is being issued during the initial distribution period. For example, since Eurobonds are not registered with the SEC, they may not be offered to any US investor during the primary marketing period. Likewise, Euroyen issues may not be sold to Japanese investors during the primary marketing period.

No specific authority regulates access to the Eurodollar market. Issuers are free to issue at any time without governmental approval. The Euroyen market is regulated by the Japanese Ministry of Finance (MOF) which imposes certain criteria regarding the size of the issue in accordance with the credit rating of the issue. The MOF may also regulate the timing of issues. The Eurosterling market is regulated by the Bank of England which must give its consent on the timing of the issue; however, this may be approved by telephone. In this market, a borrower is not permitted to raise more than £200 million in a single issue, and issues with a final maturity less than five years are prohibited. The Eurodeutschemark market is regulated by the Bundesbank which imposes restrictions similar to the Bank of England. Permission to issue is required two days prior to the issue. Other markets such as the ECU, Australian dollar and New Zealand dollar markets are not officially regulated.

The primary market

Once a borrower has decided the principal amount of funds which must be raised and the currency in which the funds will be raised, an investment bank is approached to serve as the lead manager or book runner and to arrange and underwrite the issue. The lead manager may approach other banks to underwrite a portion of the issue and participate as co-managers. It is the lead manager's and co-manager's job to sell the bonds to the investors in the primary market who include central banks, insurance companies, pension funds, private banks and fund managers. Many European banks distribute the bonds through their branch network. The managers are expected to make a two-way price in the issue, and if the bonds do not sell, the under-writers are obligated to support the issue.

Once an issue is announced, a grey market commences in the WI (when issued) market. However, the Eurobond WI is not quite the same as the WI in the treasury market. The Eurobond WI is 'when and if issued', so if for some reason the bonds are not issued, the trade is cancelled. The prices are quoted as a discount from the issue price to reflect the commissions charged on the Eurobond. Commissions will vary according to the maturity of the issue. The closing date or payment date, is the day the bonds actually come into being, usually one month after the commencement of the grey market.

The majority of Eurobonds are issued on a 'senior' basis. This means that if the borrower goes bankrupt, the holders of the bonds will not rank behind any other creditor when it comes to claiming against the borrower's assets, provided those assets have not been designated as security against another liability. If the issue is offered on a 'subordinated' basis, then the holders of the bonds will rank below the senior holders.

Settlement of Eurobonds can be either primary or secondary. Primary settlement on a new issue does not include accrued interest. Secondary settlement is one day after the closing date, so the bonds will include one day accrued interest. The bonds are delivered against payment and are normally cleared through Cedel or Euroclear.

The secondary market

Prices in the secondary market are quoted 'clean' – that is, they include no accrued interest. Accrued interest in the fixed-rate market is calculated on a 360/360 day basis, in other words, 12 months of 30 days each in a year of 360 days. Accrued interest in the floating-rate note market is calculated on a money market basis, actual/360, which means the actual number of days elapsed in a year of 360 days. The price spread will reflect the liquidity of the issue, but normally the spread in the fixed-rate market is approximately ½ a point, for example 95.50 − 96.00, and 10 to 20 ticks in the floating-rate note (FRN) market, for example 95.10 − 95.20.

Settlement in the secondary market is in seven days with the majority of bonds being cleared through Euroclear in Brussels or Cedel in Luxemburg. Most trades are settled on a 'book entry basis' providing both the buyer and the seller have an account with Euroclear or Cedel. This means the title to the bonds passes between parties without having to make physical delivery of the bonds. Instead, the bonds may be held in safe custody. However, some parties such as US, Australian and Canadian insurance companies are required by law to take physical delivery of bonds.

FIXED-RATE BONDS

Fixed-rate bonds pay a fixed rate of interest payable annually in arrears until the maturity date when the final year's interest is repaid along with the principal. This is known as a 'bullet maturity'. In the Eurodollar market, they are issued in bearer form in denominations of $1,000 and $250,000 with detachable bearer coupons. Often there is a provision known as a 'tax call' which makes the bonds redeemable in the event of the imposition of withholding taxes. However, there are many variations on the fixed-rate bond with a bullet maturity.

Putable and callable bonds

A putable bond provides the investor with the right to resell the bonds back to the issuer at par. This tends to limit how much the bonds can fall below par. A callable bond provides the issuer with the right to buy the bonds back from the investor, usually at a small premium to par.

Resettable and retractable bonds

A resettable bond allows the issuer to reset the coupon midway through the life of the bond. A coupon may be resettable more than once during the life of the bond. Often the coupons are reset period-ically in order that the bonds will trade at par. If the bond is retractable, the investor has the right to sell the bonds back to the issuer at par if the new fixed rate is unattractive.

Bonds with sinking funds

The issuer is required to redeem part of the principal on an amortizing basis.

Step-up and step-down coupon bonds

Step-up coupon bonds are those issues which begin their life carrying a coupon below the market rates, but periodically the coupon is increased so that in the later years, the coupon is set above current market levels. This appeals to investors who wish to defer their income for tax or portfolio reasons, and to borrowers who wish to pay lower tax in later years.

Step-down coupon bonds work in the opposite way. They begin their life carrying a coupon above the current market levels, and the coupon is periodically reduced to a point where the coupon is below the current market levels in later years. This appeals to investors who wish to pay lower tax in later years, and borrowers who wish to reduce their tax burden in earlier years.

Zero-coupon bonds

A zero-coupon bond is one which pays all of the interest as well as the principal repayment at maturity. Conventional bonds can be thought of as a series of zero-coupon bonds, except since interest payments are made periodically, the investor receives money quicker. Since the money is received quicker, the conventional bond has a shorter duration than the zero-coupon bond. Thus, the conventional bond will typically be less volatile than the zero-coupon bond. Furthermore, with a conventional bond the investor must bear reinvestment risk, whereas with the zero-coupon bond this is irrelevant as all funds are paid at maturity.

So, why buy a zero-coupon bond? The fact that zeros have a longer duration makes it far more likely to increase in price at a faster rate in response to lower interest rates than a conventional bond. Therefore, those investors who expect a drop in interest rates and who are seeking a capital gain from their investment will find zeros attractive. This strategy may be particularly attractive in a low inflationary period. In addition, zeros will be attractive to buy and hold investors who are unwilling to accept the reinvestment risk associated with conventional bonds.

Zero-coupon bonds first became attractive in the early 1980s mainly as a means of achieving gains through corporate tax planning in a period of high interest rates. At the time, Internal Revenue Service rules stated that the issuer of an original issue discount (OID) bond had to amortize the discount of a straight-line rather than compound-interest basis over the lifetime of the bond.[4] This translated into interest expense to the issuer and interest income to the investor. Not only was the expense to the issuer tax deductible, but because of the method of calculation, the deductible amount was larger than the true financial expense. Consequently, the firm was able to achieve a lower cost of funding. The method of calculation was changed to a compound-interest amortization in 1982 through The Tax Equity and Fiscal Responsibility Act.[5]

The Act would have killed the zero-coupon bond market were it not for the introduction in 1985 of Treasury-backed zeros or STRIPS (Separate Trading of Registered Interest and Principal of Securities) which offered no credit risk. A conventional bond is made up of a corpus representing a principal payment at maturity and a series of attached coupons, but it is possible to physically separate the unmatured coupons from the final maturity payments. A strip allows the investor to purchase one or a series of coupons. In other words, there will be separate registered owners for each of the cash flows, and thus each cash flow is sold as a separate zero-coupon instrument.

Dual currency bonds

Dual currency bonds pay coupon interest in one currency and the repayment of the principal in another currency. Usually the coupon payments are denominated in a low-interest currency such as Swiss francs or Japanese yen, and the principal repayments are in a high-interest currency such as US dollars. However, it is possible to issue a reverse dual currency bond where the interest is paid in a high interest currency and the principal repayment is paid in a low interest currency. The issuer of the dual currency bond is likely to couple the transaction with a currency swap which will ensure the foreign currency exposure is fixed.

During the 1980s, dual currency bonds were particularly targeted towards the Japanese institutional investor seeking tax arbitrage. This is discussed in more detail in Chapter 1. Dual currency markets can be an inexpensive source of US dollar financing in an environment where the investor is willing to speculate on the strength of the US dollar.

Bonds with debt warrants and equity-linked bonds (convertibles and equity warrants)

Bonds with debt warrants are fairly straightforward. In exchange for the borrower paying a lower coupon on the bond issue, the investor has the option of purchasing more bonds on fixed terms at the time of the offering of the warrants.

Convertible issues are bonds in which the principal amount is convertible into an equal amount of shares in the borrower's company. At the time of conversion, the bonds are extinguished. In return for the investor's privilege of converting the bonds to shares, the bonds normally carry a lower coupon than straight fixed-rate issues. The terms of the conversion are fixed at the outset, but in most cases the price at which the bonds are convertible is higher than the prevailing market price. The difference between the price at which the investor will receive the shares upon conversion and the price of the shares at launch is known as the 'conversion premium'. In addition, convertible bonds are normally callable by the issuer after two to three years at a large premium. The issuer may also call the bond if the shares in the company have traded at a price greater than or equal to 130% of the conversion price for a period of 30–60 days. In this event, the investor is unlikely to accept the call on the bonds, because it would be beneficial to convert the bonds to shares. This is referred to as a 'forced conversion'. Occasionally, convertibles are putable by the investors at a premium to par which provides the investors with downside protection if the shares in the borrower's company do not perform well.

Some Eurobonds have equity warrants attached, which is effectively an option to buy shares at a predetermined price in the issuing company. Normally, the bond will carry a lower coupon reflecting this option. The right to buy the shares is detachable from the bond, and the warrants may be traded separately. The price of the warrant is the 'warrant premium' which is 100 minus the price of the bond quoted as a percentage. In other words, if the bond price is 97.00, then the warrant premium would be 3%. The exercise premium is the difference between the price of the shares at launch and the price of the shares at which the investor may buy the shares. Unlike the terms of a convertible bond, equity warrants may provide for the purchase of a lesser amount of shares than the principal on the bonds. For example, if an investor owns $100 million in bonds, the investor may be entitled to purchase only $50 million in shares. This is known as the 'warrantability' of the issue. If the warrants are exercised, the bonds continue to trade as normal.

FLOATING-RATE NOTES

In the 1970s volatile inflation rates and interest rates were causing a loss to investors on fixed-rate securities. In response, the floating-rate note (FRN) was born. This instrument provided for a coupon rate reset on specified rollover dates, usually three-monthly or six-monthly, and usually as a fixed spread over LIBOR. Banks and finance companies were keen to issue the new instrument as the cash flows naturally matched their asset portfolios. While FRNs offer greater protection for the investor against interest rate risk, credit risk remains.

In the US dollar market, FRNs are normally issued in denominations of $5,000 and $25,000 with a fixed maturity date. However, it is possible to issue a 'perpetual' FRN, which is one with no fixed maturity date. Most FRNs are callable at par, usually after two or three years subject to the regulations of the specific markets in which the issue was made.

Floating-rate notes can also be structured as inverse FRNs. In other words, the FRN will pay a percentage minus LIBOR. These may be coupled with interest rate swaps in order to achieve a lower all-in cost of funds calculated as:

$$(percentage - LIBOR) + (LIBOR - fixed\ rate\ on\ the\ swap)$$
$$= all\text{-}in\ cost\ of\ funds$$

ASSET SWAPS

Asset swaps are swaps attached to an asset or portfolio of assets that modify the cash flows either in terms of coupon, timing, currency or a mixture of these. The reason one may want to enter into an asset swap is to tailor a portfolio to the individual's requirements by changing fixed cash flows into floating cash flows, floating cash flows into fixed cash flows or cash flows in one currency into cash flows in another. They may eliminate funding/liability mismatches and maturity mismatches.

An asset swap may enable the portfolio manager to lock in arbitrage opportunities. The growth of the asset swap market was spurred by commercial bank demand for good quality banking assets, but at the same time there was a demand for cash-flow restructuring to fit the banks' portfolios.

Before entering into an asset swap, one should ensure that the covenants on the debt issues match those on the swap. For example, FRNs frequently contain a material adverse change clause which enables the borrower to shorten the maturity of the debt. Against this, the investor might want to enter into a callable swap.

Creation of a synthetic FRN

The investor buys, or has in a portfolio, a non-callable, investment grade bond upon which he receives a fixed-coupon payment. The

FIGURE 4.1   Creation of a synthetic FRN

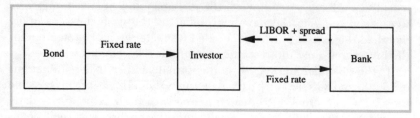

investor enters into a swap, to pay the fixed rate to a counterparty, and in turn receive the floating rate, which is usually a spread over LIBOR. The maturity of the swap is matched with the maturity of the bond, so when the bond is redeemed, the swap terminates as well. By changing the fixed payments into floating payments, the investor may be able to take advantage of rising interest rates at a time when the price of the fixed-rate bond may be falling. (See Figure 4.1.)

Creation of a synthetic fixed instrument

This works in the same way as the above example. The investor buys, or has in a portfolio, a non-callable, investment grade bond upon which a floating coupon payment is received. The investor enters into a swap to pay the floating rate to the counterparty and receive the fixed rate. The maturity of the swap is matched with the maturity of the bond, so when the bond is redeemed, the swap terminates as well. This allows the investor to lock in a higher yield at a time when interest rates are falling. (See Figure 4.2.)

Existing asset repackaging

Several underlying bonds with different coupon payment dates and maturities can be repackaged by attaching an asset swap which converts the many fixed flows into semi-annual floating-rate payments

FIGURE 4.2   Creation of a synthetic fixed instrument

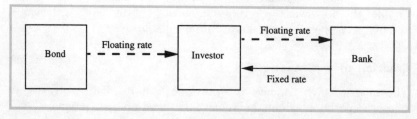

that are passed on to the purchasers of the repackaged FRNs. A holding company is set up to own the underlying bonds. The holding company issues the repackaged FRNs and enters into the swap.

Arbitrage opportunities using asset swaps

An issuer raises funds in the fixed-rate market. The issuer then enters into a swap to receive fixed and pay floating with a sub-LIBOR structure. The two fixed payments net off, and the issuer is left raising funds at sub-LIBOR. The issuer uses the funds that were raised in the market to purchase a portfolio of fixed-rate bonds in the market. The issuer enters into a second swap whereby the fixed coupon payments are passed to the counterparty, and the issuer receives a floating rate, usually LIBOR plus a spread. The aim is for the issuer to purchase assets that yield LIBOR plus a spread, and finance that position at sub-LIBOR.

The advantages and disadvantages of using asset swaps

There are many advantages of asset swaps. As with swaps in general, it provides the portfolio manager with a flexible vehicle to achieve his or her objectives. In particular, there may be a window of opportunity to make a better return than investing in the bond alone. In addition, it enables the user to spread credit risk or sovereign risk by diversifying into names not seen in the bond market. Furthermore, lead managers of equity warrant issues sometimes can use asset swaps to repackage the ex-warrant bonds left on their books.

Of course, there are also disadvantages in using this product. First, the user must accept double credit risk – that is, on the bond issuer and on the swap counterparty. Second, the asset swap market is not a liquid one, so disposing of the package may be difficult.

LIABILITY SWAPS (FORWARD, CALLABLE AND PUTABLE)

The risk profile of a firm will have an impact on the value of the firm, thus it is essential to establish an optimal risk profile. The determination of the risk profile involves questioning whether the firm is likely to be able to bear the risk of covering all of its costs under any circumstances versus somehow reducing those risks through hedging. To answer this question, the treasurer must draw up several cash budgets assuming different economic conditions and levels of hedging to reduce risk. If the treasurer feels an alteration is necessary, two possible alternatives available are to lower the gearing of the firm or to hedge the existing liabilities.

One can gain insights into investors' expectations of returns given a level of risk by looking at modern financial theories such as the Capital Asset Pricing Model (CAPM) and the Arbitrage Pricing Theory (APT). In theory, hedging will increase or at least sustain the value of the firm in the face of 'total risk' or the total variability of the firm's cash flows. It can be argued that if a firm does not hedge, it is more likely that the operating side of the business will suffer, and thus there is more likely to be a negative impact on the future cash flows. This may lead to a snowball effect which will destroy management, employee and customer confidence, followed by a drop in sales and ultimately poor returns to the shareholders or even bankruptcy.

The decision whether or not to issue debt in the first place will depend on specific industry norms, the state of the corporate debt market in general and the firm's current debt/equity ratio. The treasurer will watch the yields and ratings on the firm's corporate debt for indications as to how the market perceives the company's current risk profile. Once the treasurer has decided to issue debt, the aim is to achieve the lowest cost of funds possible. To achieve this goal, there are several financial products available to the treasurer who decides to hedge existing liabilities or reduce the firm's funding costs, but one way of accomplishing this task is by using interest rate swaps.

Liability swaps are similar to asset swaps except one must look at them from the issuer's perspective. They provide the issuer with flexibility to reduce the cost of funding, while taking advantage of changing market conditions. The borrower may modify the interest payments due in the same way as an investor can with asset swaps by changing a floating structure into a fixed structure and vice versa. Issuers can lock in the cost on an expected future borrowing requirement. The issuer may also be able to take advantage of arbitrage opportunities.

The decision whether to hedge a liability using swaps will depend on market sentiment and the shape of the yield curve. For example, if the yield curve is inverted, it may be unwise to lock into a high borrowing cost for a long period when interest rates are likely to fall in the near future. On the other hand, if a treasurer expects interest rates to fall slowly, a swap with a short maturity will produce a positive carry. Furthermore, prior to swapping the treasurer must consider whether attractive swap pricing is available for the desired maturity, whether there will be better opportunities in the future to fix borrowing costs, whether spreads on new issues are lower than swap spreads, and whether an overall adjustment is required in the ratio of fixed-to-floating rate debt.

Like asset swaps, the treasurer should endeavour to match the covenants on the issue with the swap. For example, one pitfall might occur in conjunction with an FRN with a minimum coupon rate. Suppose the firm has issued an FRN with a minimum coupon of 5% coupled with an interest rate swap changing the structure to a fixed exposure. In the unlikely event that LIBOR drops to 4%, the firm will lose 1% as it will be paying out 5% on the FRN and only receiving 4% from the swap. In this case, if the firm can afford the premium, the treasurer may consider buying a 5% floor.[6]

Forward swaps

Forward swaps are swaps which are transacted today to commence sometime in the future. These can be useful if hedging future payments or income streams which are known in advance. Forward swaps provide the portfolio manager or corporate treasurer with a certain degree of flexibility in liability management, and if there is a profit on the forward swap, the treasurer takes this into account when calculating the sub-LIBOR spread on a new issue.

Cash settlement forward swaps are a recent development in this area. Here, a forward swap agreement is put into place at time A to begin at time B. However, instead of the actual swap beginning, a cash settlement takes place between the counterparties based on the net present value of the transaction at time B. This process is very similar to the one used to close out an existing swap transaction, to assign an existing swap transaction, and to cash settle a swap option.

There are four main reasons why a portfolio manager might use a forward swap:

1. Lengthening the maturity of existing fixed-rate debt.
2. Locking in a financing or refinancing rate on anticipated or callable debt.
3. Shortening the maturity structure of long-term fixed-rate debt.
4. Removing sensitivities from a portfolio of debt.

Lengthening the maturity of existing fixed-rate debt

In this instance, suppose a firm has issued debt for five years, but a couple of years into the issue, the treasurer feels that it may be necessary to extend that maturity to seven years. A forward swap may be entered into whereby the firm pays a fixed rate for two years, five

FIGURE 4.3 Lengthening the maturity of existing fixed-rate debt

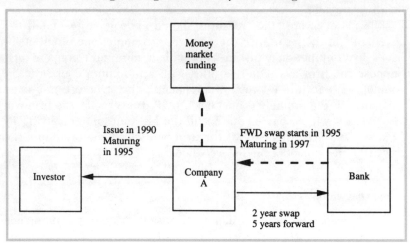

years forward. This is not literally extending the debt, but it will extend the fixed-rate aspect of the debt. (See Figure 4.3.)

Locking in a financing or refinancing rate on anticipated or callable debt

In this case a firm may wish to enter into a forward swap to lock in a beneficial interest rate for the future when a project is in the pipeline. For example, suppose a company is going to enter into a building project which is to commence in two years' time and finish in five years' time, and a loan account will be provided by the bank for the firm to draw-down funds according to a schedule. The treasurer may arrange a forward swap where the company pays a fixed rate to commence in two years and run for three years to parallel the loan account. (See Figure 4.4.)

Likewise, suppose a firm has issued a callable bond, and interest rates have dropped since the issue. The treasurer may take the opportunity to refinance through the swap market by using a forward swap. The start date of the swap would be the call date on the bond, and the maturity of the swap would be the maturity of the bond. (See Figure 4.5.)

Shortening the maturity structure of long-term fixed-rate debt

When interest rates are low, companies prefer to lengthen the maturities of their fixed-rate debt; however, when interest rates are high they prefer to shorten the maturities. For example, suppose a company

FIGURE 4.4   Locking in a financing or refinancing rate on
anticipated debt

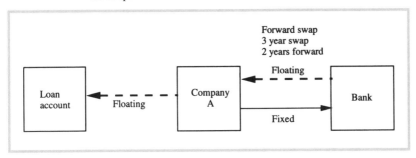

issued five-year fixed-rate debt, but two years after issuing the debt
interest rates started to rise. If the treasurer feels that rates will rise
further for the next year and then start to decline, then the company
may enter into a swap transaction which will effectively cancel out the
fixed-rate liability at a time when interest rates are falling by transacting a forward swap commencing in one year to receive the fixed rate
for two years up to the maturity of the bond and pay the floating rate.
(See Figure 4.6.)

Removing sensitivities from a portfolio of debt

In the examples above, it was discussed how a treasurer may want to
lengthen or shorten the maturity of a bond, or lock in financing or

FIGURE 4.5   Locking in financing on callable debt

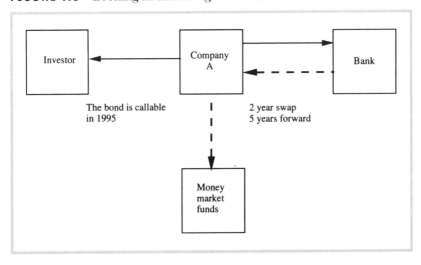

FIGURE 4.6 Shortening the maturity structure of long-term fixed-rate debt

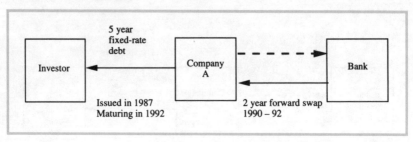

refinancing. The same can be done for a portfolio of bonds. Forward swaps are another tool to be used in managing risk in a swap portfolio. They can be used to shorten or lengthen the duration of a portfolio, for example.

Structuring and pricing of forward swaps

Suppose a company wishes to pay fixed in a two-year swap three years forward – a three- against a five-year swap. The bank or intermediary will hedge the deal by paying five years and receiving three years, and the price for the forward swap will reflect the cost of this hedge, or the amount needed to recoup a negative cash flow in the first years. If it is a normal yield curve – that is, forward rates are higher than nearby rates – then the bank will charge a premium over the straight five-year swap rate, because the bank will be receiving a lower rate for three years and paying a higher rate for five years. If the yield curve is inverted, then the bank will charge a discount to the straight five-year rate, reflecting the higher rate being received for three years and the lower rate being paid for five years. The premium or discount is the present value of the difference between the two rates (per annum) projected into the future plus a profit margin.

For example, suppose Company A wishes to enter into a forward swap whereby it pays in a two-year swap three years forward. The swap rate will reflect the bank's cost of hedging the transaction which will be to receive in a three-year swap and pay in a five-year swap. For our purposes here, let us assume that the bank will receive three years at 7.68% and pay five years at 8.28% (see Figure 4.7). Table 4.1 shows what the bank's cash flows will look like.

Essentially, the bank must recover a loss of 60 basis points per annum from years 1, 2 and 3 in years 4 and 5. By using a spread sheet or a financial calculator, one can determine this rate in two steps:

FIGURE 4.7 Diagram of a forward swap

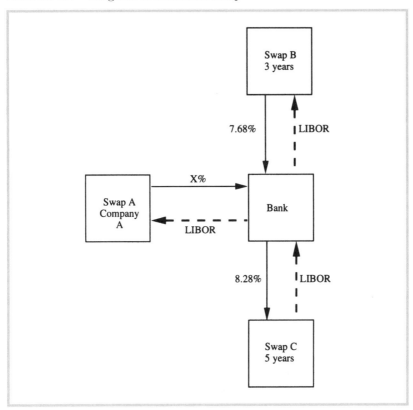

1. Calculate the future value of 60 basis points spread over 3 periods at 7.68%.

2. Calculate the annual payment this would represent over 2 periods with a present value equal to the future value as above at 8.28%.

The payment is added on to the current 5-year swap rate, so in this case 109 basis points will be added to 8.28% to give the forward swap rate at 9.37%.

The advantages and disadvantages of using forward swaps

Forward swaps can be advantageous in that they provide the user with flexibility. They are often cost efficient, they are an off-balance sheet item, and they may provide the company with a way of avoiding having to access the capital markets when it is not beneficial to do so. As with

TABLE 4.1 The bank's cash flows

Year	1	2	3	4	5
Swap A	–	–	–	+X	+X
				−L	−L
Swap B	7.68	7.68	7.68	–	–
	−L	−L	−L		
Swap C	−8.28	−8.28	−8.28	−8.28	−8.28
	+L	+L	+L	+L	+L
Total	−0.60	−0.60	−0.60	X − 8.28	X − 8.28

Note: The bank will receive 3 years at 7.68% and pay 5 years at 8.28%.

all swaps, risk can never totally be eliminated. Therefore, the user may be exposed to liquidity and credit risk.

Callable swaps

A callable swap gives the payer the right to terminate the swap at a particular point in time. Callable swaps can be used to transform callable debt into non-callable debt, and to transform callable debt into floating-rate debt. However, they are only cost effective when the bond market prices the embedded call option more cheaply than the swap market.

Transforming callable debt into non-callable debt

For example, Company A may issue fixed-rate debt with a 10-year maturity callable in five years. Effectively, the issuer has bought a call and thus will be paying a higher coupon rate then a straight five-year issue. The issuer can change this to non-callable debt by entering into two swaps. The first swap will be a 10-year swap callable in five years, whereby the issuer receives the fixed rate and pays the floating rate. The swap counterparty will pay a premium over the straight swap rate reflecting the right to terminate the swap. Effectively, the issuer has sold a call. The issuer then enters into a second swap, a straight 10-year, this time paying the fixed rate and receiving the floating rate. (See Figure 4.8.)

As a result, for the first five years, Company A will pay fixed-rate interest as normal, however, the cost of funding will be reduced by the premium received on the callable swap. If interest rates move higher, the issuer will not choose to call the bond, because the firm will have to refinance at a higher rate. Nor will the swap payer call the swap,

FIGURE 4.8 Transforming callable debt into non-callable debt using callable swaps

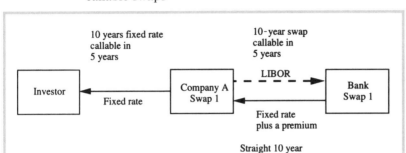

because the swap will be in-the-money. However, if interest rates move lower, then the issuer will call the bond in order to refinance at a lower rate. In turn, the callable swap counterparty will call the swap. The issuer can borrow floating-rate funds in the money market, which will automatically be swapped to a fixed rate by way of the straight swap which will remain in place.

Transforming callable debt into floating-rate debt

Company A has issued 10-year fixed-rate debt callable in five years. This time, Company A enters into one 10-year swap callable in five years as a receiver of the fixed rate and payer of the floating rate. As in the previous example, the swap counterparty will have to pay a premium for the privilege of calling the swap. This premium may reduce the borrowing cost to sub-LIBOR for Company A. Thus, the issuer has swapped the fixed-rate debt into floating-rate debt. If interest rates move higher, the bond and the swap will remain in place. However, if interest rates move lower, Company A will call the bond,

FIGURE 4.9 Transforming callable debt into floating-rate debt

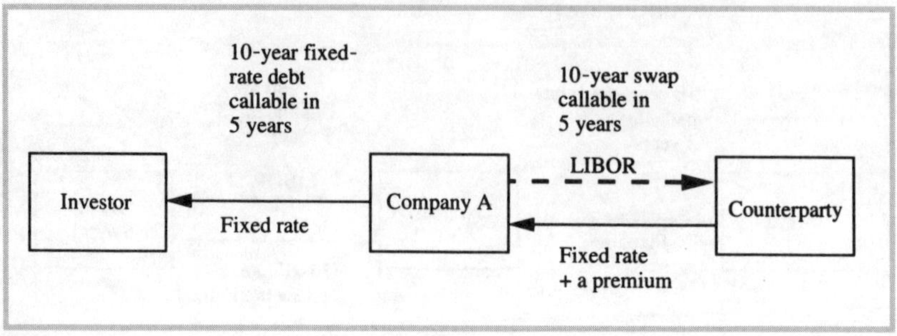

and the counterparty will call the swap. Company A can fund floating in the money market. (See Figure 4.9.)

Putable swaps

Putable swaps give the receiver in the swap the right to terminate the swap at a specific period in time. Putable swaps can be used in a similar way to callable swaps. The cost effectiveness of this structure rests on the assumption that the bond market prices the embedded put option more dearly than the swap market.

Transforming putable debt into non-putable fixed-rate debt

For example, Company A has issued a 10-year fixed rate bond, putable in five years. This means the investor has the right to sell the bond back to the issuer, so the company will be paying a lower coupon rate reflecting the investor's privilege. Company A can enter into a 10-year swap putable in five years as a receiver of the fixed rate and payer of the floating rate. Company A will receive a lower fixed rate than a straight five-year swap to reflect the ability to terminate the swap. In turn, Company A can enter into a second straight 10-year swap as a payer of the fixed rate and a receiver of the floating rate. (See Figure 4.10.)

For the first five years Company A will have received fixed funding. If by the put date interest rates have moved lower, then all will remain intact. The investor will not want to sell the bonds back to the issuer, because the investment will be making a return. However, if interest rates move higher, then the investor will sell the bonds back to Company A in order to reinvest at a higher rate. Company A will put the swap back to the counterparty. Company A can fund floating in the money market and swap this back to a fixed rate through the second straight 10-year swap.

FIGURE 4.10   Transforming putable debt into non-putable fixed-rate debt

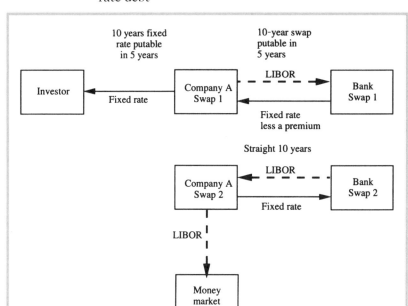

Transforming putable debt into floating-rate debt

This structure works in the same way as in the example on the callable debt. Company A issues a 10-year fixed rate bond, putable in five years. This is coupled with a 10-year swap putable in five years, whereby Company A pays the floating rate and receives a fixed rate. The fixed rate will be lower than the straight 10-year swap rate reflecting Company A's right to terminate the swap, but it should be higher than the coupon rate on the bond. This will provide Company A with sub-LIBOR funding for the first five years. If interest rates go lower, both the bond and the swap will remain intact. If interest rates move higher, the investor will put the bond back to Company A. Company A will terminate the swap and fund floating in the money market. (See Figure 4.11.)

SUMMARY

The Eurobond market began in the late 1950s, but it grew at a phenomenal rate in the 1970s and 1980s as firms sought a way to

FIGURE 4.11   Transforming putable debt into floating-rate debt

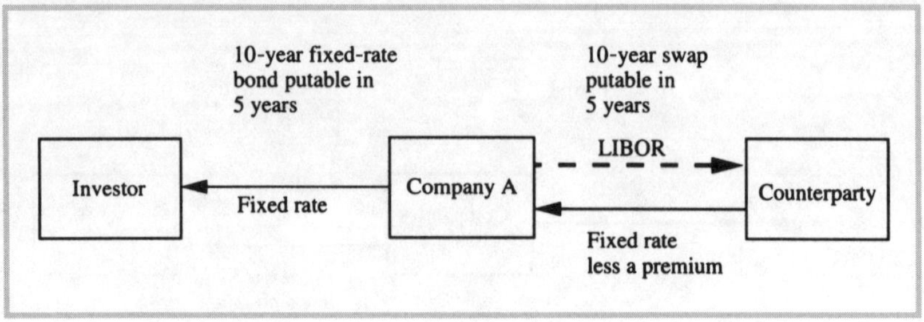

circumvent regulations in the domestic market. During the 1980s, the wave of corporate restructuring in the form of takeovers, divestment and recapitalization was reason to provide a healthy supply of corporate bonds. At the same time, there was strong demand on the part of the investor to buy both investment grade bonds and 'junk' bonds. The Eurobond market provided both the borrower and the investor with a wider base for raising and investing funds.

In order to attract investors and at the same time provide flexibility for the borrower, there are several structures of Eurobonds including putable and callable bonds, resettable and retractable bonds, bonds with sinking funds, step-up and step-down coupon bonds, zero-coupon bonds, dual currency bonds, bonds with debt warrants and equity-linked bonds and floating-rate notes. All of these bonds may be combined with swaps which provides flexibility for both the investor and the borrower. Asset swaps are swaps used by investors to change the structure of a bond being held in a portfolio. For example, the portfolio manager may create a synthetic FRN or a synthetic fixed instrument. Liability swaps are swaps used by borrowers to change the terms of their bond issues. For example, the treasurer may use forward swaps, callable swaps or putable swaps against the company's bond issues or loan accounts.

Notes

1. In this case, the issuer could deduct the discount amortization from the annual tax bill.

2. Donald J. Smith and Robert A. Taggert. 'Bond market innovations and financial intermediation', *Business Horizons*, November/December 1989, p. 27.

3. Donald J. Smith and Robert A. Taggert, op. cit., p. 26.

4. An OID bond is one in which the issue price is less than 100 minus 0.25 times the number of years to maturity. See Donald J. Smith and Robert A. Taggert, op. cit., p. 33.

5. Donald J. Smith and Robert A. Taggert, op. cit., p. 28.

6. This is based on an example in the article by Donald J. Smith, 'Measuring the gains from arbitraging the swap market', *Financial Executive*, vol. 4, March/April 1988, pp. 48–9.

Bibliography

Antl, Boris (ed.) (1986). *Swap Finance, Vols I and II*. London: Euromoney Publications Ltd.

Das, Satyajit (1989). *Swap Financing*. London: IFR Publishing Ltd.

DeCovny, Sherree and Tacchi, Christine (1991). *Hedging Strategies*. Cambridge: Woodhead-Faulkner (Publishers) Ltd.

Goodman, Laurie S. (1990). 'The use of interest rate swaps in managing corporate liabilities', *Continental Bank Journal of Applied Corporate Finance*, Continental Bank, vol. 2, winter, pp. 35–48.

Henderson, Schuyler K. and Price, John A. M. (1988). *Currency and Interest Rate Swaps*, 2nd edition. London: Butterworths.

Ireland, Louise (1988). 'Getting a fix with swaps', *Corporate Finance*, no. 47, October, pp. 39, 42.

May, Michael (1990). 'To swap or not to swap', *The Treasurer*, vol. 12, no. 2, February, pp. 14–20.

Shapiro, A. C. and Titman, S. (1985). 'An integrated approach to corporate risk management', *Midland Corporate Finance Journal*, summer, pp. 41–56.

Smith, Donald J. (1988). 'Measuring the gains from arbitraging the swap market', *Financial Executive*, vol. 4, March/April, pp. 46–9.

Smith, Donald J. and Taggert, Robert A. (1989). 'Bond market innovations and financial intermediation', *Business Horizons*, November/December, pp. 24–34.

VARIATIONS ON THE SWAP THEME

5

As the swap market grew, and swap users learned to apply various forms of technical analysis to the swap product, a number of swap structures became more common for use in risk management. Some structures are extremely simple, such as the basis swap. Others are more complex such as amortizing swaps, roller-coaster swaps, off-market coupon swaps, LIBOR-in-arrears swaps, participation swaps and zero-coupon swaps. Option products such as caps, floors, collars and swaptions have developed, and are now widely used risk management tools.

BASIS SWAPS

Basis swaps involve an exchange of floating-rate payments calculated on different bases. The structure of a basis swap is the same as the straight interest rate swap, with the exception that floating interest calculated on one basis is exchanged for floating interest calculated on a different basis. Examples of basis swaps include LIBOR-LIBOR (3-month against 6-month, etc.), Prime-LIBOR and CP-LIBOR.

A basis swap can be quite useful in ensuring that payments are on the same basis as receivables. It allows an entity to arbitrage spreads between different floating rate funding sources. Perhaps the most common usage is to solve mismatches in a portfolio. In terms of risk, basis rate swaps are the simplest type of swap and subject the counterparties to the least amount of potential exposure. This is because they involve the exchange of two floating-rate sums based on two short-term interest rate benchmarks, usually in the same currency. The main risk is the potential change in spread differentials.

LIBOR-LIBOR

This type of swap can be used for various reasons. Two examples are as follows:

1. A bank may want to enter into a plain vanilla swap to pay the fixed rate and receive 3-month LIBOR, but only a swap rate against 6-month LIBOR is quoted. The swap can be transacted against 6-month LIBOR, and later a basis swap may be entered into whereby the bank pays 6-month LIBOR and receives 3-month LIBOR, therefore solving the mismatch in the portfolio. (See Figure 5.1.)

2. This type of swap can be entered into when a portfolio manager feels that differentials between different LIBORs will change. For example, if it is likely that the spread between 1-month LIBOR and 6-month LIBOR will narrow, the portfolio manager will enter into a basis swap to receive 1-month LIBOR and pay 6-month LIBOR. (See Figure 5.2.)

Prime-LIBOR

This was one of the first types of basis swaps to appear in the market. The need for such a structure arose, because US banks had substantial LIBOR-priced assets which they could fund more profitably on a prime basis, and European banks preferred to have LIBOR-priced assets as opposed to prime-priced assets. Therefore, by accessing the swap market, the US and European banks could enter more freely into

FIGURE 5.1 LIBOR-LIBOR basis swap: pay 6-month LIBOR and receive 3-month LIBOR

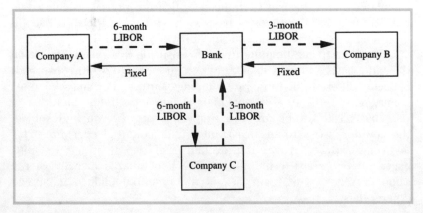

FIGURE 5.2 LIBOR-LIBOR basis swap: receive 1-month LIBOR and pay 6-month LIBOR

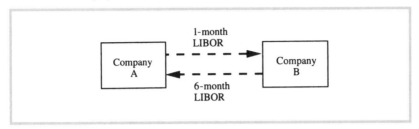

syndicated loans without being at a disadvantage when it came down to financing the loan. (See Figure 5.3.)

CP-LIBOR

This structure provides an efficient method for European entities in particular to simulate the US commercial paper funding market without having to meet the stringent requirements for a commercial paper programme. Under this scenario, the European company would borrow money at LIBOR, pay CP in the swap and receive LIBOR from the counterparty. The two LIBORs would net off and the European firm would be left paying the CP rate. CP-LIBOR spreads historically run at an average differential of 90 basis points with the minimum being 50 basis points and the maximum being 150 basis points. (See Figure 5.4.)

FIGURE 5.3 Prime-LIBOR basis swap

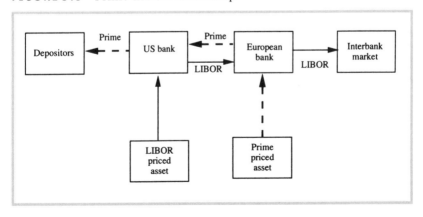

FIGURE 5.4 CP-LIBOR basis swap

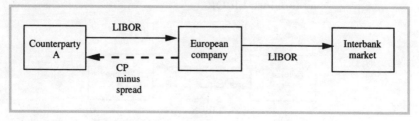

AMORTIZING SWAPS

Amortizing swaps are very popular for lease-based transactions where the principal reduces annually or even more frequently. For example, suppose Company A has borrowed $9 million to buy a building. It has agreed with its bankers to pay back the loan, principal plus interest at 8.50% fixed, over 3 years. Company A thinks that interest rates are going to fall over the period, and thus would prefer to pay a floating rate rather than a fixed rate. Company A can enter into a swap with the bank in which the notional principal decreases on each of the amortization dates. (See Figure 5.5.)

The price of the swap quoted to Company A will be determined by how the bank hedges the amortizing swap. In this example (see Figure 5.6), the bank can accomplish this by receiving in three swaps, each written for $3 million maturing in 1 year, 2 years and 3 years. The rates in this case are:

1 year 7.00% A/360[1]
2 years 7.30% A/360
3 years 7.72% A/360

FIGURE 5.5 An amortizing swap

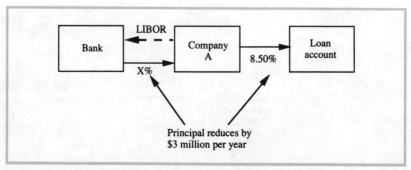

FIGURE 5.6 The bank hedges the amortizing swap

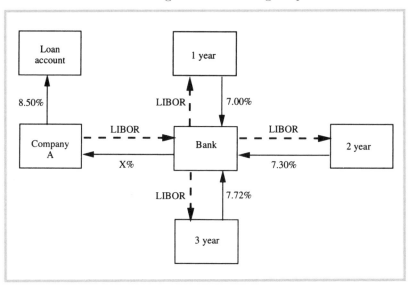

The coupon on the swap will be the internal rate of return of the cash flows generated from the three swaps. Each year, one of the swaps will mature, as follows:

			Swaps	
Year	1	2		3
1	7.00	7.30		7.72
2		7.30		7.72
3				7.72

Therefore the cash flows will be:

Y/E 0	(9,000,000)
Y/E 1	3,669,776
Y/E 2	3,456,859
Y/E 3	3,234,817
IRR (and swap rate)^2	7.56%

ROLLER-COASTER SWAPS

A variation on the amortizing swap is the roller-coaster swap where the principal involved increases and decreases over the life of the swap.

For example, suppose Company A's project requires a total principal of $20 million over 5 years. Instead of paying back an equal $4 million per year, Company A's project will allow a repayment of $5 million at the end of year 1, $4 million at the end of year 2, $3 million at the end of year 3, $5 million at the end of year 4 and $3 million at the end of year 5. As in the amortizing swap, the coupon rate on the swap will be the internal rate of return of the cash flows generated from five swaps. The following table shows how each year one of the swaps will mature:

Year	1	2	Swaps 3	4	5
1	7.00	7.30	7.72	8.02	8.28
2		7.30	7.32	8.02	8.28
3			7.32	8.02	8.28
4				8.02	8.28
5					8.28

Therefore the cash flows will be:

Y/E 0	(20,000,000)
Y/E 1	6,544,153
Y/E 2	5,189,292
Y/E 3	3,893,236
Y/E 4	5,658,419
Y/E 5	3,251,850
IRR (and swap rate)	7.94%

LIBOR ADJUSTMENTS AND OFF-MARKET COUPONS

An off-market coupon or non-par value swap is one which has a fixed rate above or below the current market rate. In this case, an up-front payment is made which is equal to the present value of the annuity based on the difference between the off-market coupon swap rate and the current market rate, multiplied by the notional principal amount.[3]

For example, this type of swap can be structured to fit in with existing borrowings. A company may want to set a swap rate equivalent to the coupon rate on a debt issue. If a company has existing borrowings at a spread over LIBOR, an interest rate swap can be structured to match this. An adjustment would simply be made to the fixed rate payable. If the annual money market fixed rate for a 5-year US dollar swap was 8.25% per annum against receiving 6-month LIBOR, 8.50% would be payable against receiving LIBOR plus ¼%.

An off-market coupon swap may also be done in conjunction with an up-front payment. For example, a firm has previously issued $10 million of 9.00% fixed-rate debt which matures in 4 years, but now wants to swap this into a floating-rate liability. Let us suppose that the current 4-year swap rate is 8.08%, but Company A wants to set the coupon rate on the swap at 9.00%, so the receipt on the swap will exactly match the payment on the bond. In return for receiving an above-the-market coupon rate on the swap, Company A will make an up-front payment to the bank equal to the present value of 0.92%, being $0.0900 - 0.0808$, multiplied by the notional principal over 4 years. Thus, $0.0092 \times 10,000,000 = 92,000$. The net present value of 92,000 per year over 4 years discounted at the current swap rate is $304,173.85, which will be the up-front payment in return for receiving 9.00% on the swap and paying LIBOR flat.

LIBOR-IN-ARREARS SWAPS

In a generic swap, LIBOR is normally set six months and two days before a payment date; however, it is possible to structure a swap so that LIBOR is fixed two days before the payment date. This structure may be advantageous when the yield curve is positively sloped and the implied forward rates are higher than the physical yield curve, but at the same time the swap user expects that short-term rates will remain stable or decrease.

PARTICIPATION SWAPS

The participation swap is a hybrid product, which incorporates the advantages of the swap and cap/floor products. Under this arrangement, an interest rate swap is transacted to cover a portion of the notional principal, and an interest rate cap is transacted to cover the remainder of the notional principal. The fixed rate on the swap and the strike price on the cap are identical. The term and periodicity of the cap and swap are also identically matched. There is no up-front premium payable.

If LIBOR is set above the cap/swap strike price, then the counterparty must pay the user the difference between LIBOR and the strike price on the total notional principal. In other words, the participation swap behaves like a cap. Thus, the borrower can effectively fix his borrowing cost for all of the exposure.

On the other hand, if LIBOR is set at a rate lower than cap/swap strike price, then the transaction functions as a swap only on the swap portion of the notional principal. Consequently, the user may still achieve a lower rate on a proportion of the notional principal. This proportion remains constant for any LIBOR fixing below the cap/swap level, and is known as the degree of participation. Thus, a participation swap is used when interest rates could rise but the treasurer also wants some benefit if rates fall.

For example, suppose the current 4-year sterling interest rate swap is offered at 12.64% semi-annual versus 6-month LIBOR, and the interest rate cap with a strike price of 12.64% against 6-month LIBOR is offered at 116 basis points, including protection for the first 6 months. It is possible to obtain a 50% participation swap on a notional principal of £10,000,000 at 13.22%.

Each time LIBOR is set above 13.22% on the rollover date, the participation swap will behave as a cap for the full £10,000,000. Each time LIBOR is set below 13.22%, the user will be obligated to pay the fixed rate of 13.22% and receive the LIBOR rate only on a notional principal of £5,000,000. The remaining £5,000,000 may be funded at the current market level incurring no further cost.

In the case of 50% participation, the user achieves an overall funding rate halfway between the prevailing LIBOR rate and the participation swap rate, for LIBOR settings below that of the participation swap. As the degree of participation varies, so does the weighting of the overall funding cost in relation to LIBOR and the swap rate. Thus, a 25% participation swap would provide the user with 25% of the benefit of LIBOR rates below that of the swap rate. It is possible to create varying levels of participation, and one may obtain a lower swap strike level the lower the level of participation.[4]

ZERO-COUPON SWAPS

Like a zero-coupon bond, the payer in a zero-coupon swap will make only one fixed payment at maturity. The ultimate fixed payment is a single forward rate based on the compounding of the immediate cash flows at the swap rate. This structure is most commonly used in conjunction with zero-coupon bond issues, so the issuer's net cash flow is almost identical to what it would have been if it had issued a low-cost coupon floating-rate instrument. For example, a borrower could issue a zero-coupon bond and enter into a matching zero-coupon swap whereby it receives a fixed rate, which will ultimately offset the payment to the bondholders on maturity, and in turn pays a floating rate.

While there is no reinvestment risk on a zero-coupon swap, from the floating rate payer's point of view, the credit risk on a zero-coupon swap is higher than the credit risk on a generic swap. This is because the floating-rate payer will receive only one payment at maturity while having to make periodic payments under the swap agreement. If the fixed-rate payer defaults, potentially the floating-rate payer will be unable to recover the interest payments it has already made.

SWAP OPTIONS

A swap option or 'swaption' is an option on a swap which gives the buyer the right but not the obligation to enter into an interest rate swap with a fixed rate equal to the strike price on the option. The swap option counterparties must agree a start date and a maturity date as well as all the specific details of the underlying swap. Swap options may be traded either European-style, exercisable on one date only, or American-style, exercisable at any time up to and including the maturity date. Premiums are quoted in flat basis points of the notional swap principal.

The buyer of an interest rate swap option has the right to enter into an interest rate swap contract with the option writer on a deliverable or non-deliverable basis. A deliverable basis means that if on the maturity date the option is exercised, the counterparties enter into an actual swap. A non-deliverable basis means that if on the maturity date the option is exercised, there is a cash settlement. Non-deliverable swap options are currently preferred, because the shorter term carries less credit risk.

While swap options function in the same way as puts and calls, the terminology associated with swap options differs from other options. Given the complexity of the interest rate swap contract, it is less ambiguous to refer to swap option contracts as payer's swap options and receiver's swap options. A buyer of a payer's option has the right to pay the fixed rate and receive the floating rate. The buyer of a receiver's option has the right to receive the fixed rate and pay the floating rate. A payer's option may also be referred to as a back-end fixed swaption, and a receiver's option may be referred to as a back-end floating swaption, although these terms are less commonly used.

For example, suppose a treasurer has a five-year fixed-rate funding requirement contingent on the acceptance of a tender, and the acceptance date for the tender is in six months. A forward swap contract could prove costly if the tender is unsuccessful. An alternative for the treasurer is to buy a payer's swaption with an exercise date matching the date of acceptance on the tender. If rates increase in the interim, the firm may raise floating-rate funds in the money market and at the same time exercise the in-the-money swaption. Once the swaption has been exercised, the firm will have the right to enter an interest rate swap with the option writer to pay the fixed rate and receive LIBOR for five years. If rates are unchanged or decline, the option will expire, and the treasurer may fund at a lower rate.

The above example shows how a treasurer with a contingent liability may use an interest rate swaption to secure protection against an increase in interest rates. An asset manager holding a floating-rate note in the portfolio may use a receiver's swaption to hedge against declining rates. If the asset manager anticipates that in six months interest rates will decline, a receiver's swaption exercisable in six months may be bought to hedge against the decline in rates. If interest rates remain unchanged or increase, the option will expire unexercised. If interest rates decline, the asset manager will exercise the swap, thus converting the floating-rate asset into a fixed-rate asset.

A variation on the swap option is the putable and callable swap. These are swaps in which one of the counterparties has the right to terminate the swap on a given date. In a callable swap, the fixed-rate payer has the right to terminate the transaction on a given date. To reflect the embedded call option, the fixed rate is higher than the straight swap rate for that particular maturity. In a putable swap, the receiver has the right to terminate the transaction, thus the fixed rate is lower than the straight swap rate reflecting the embedded put option. Putable and callable swaps are used in conjunction with bond issues. For more information on these structures, see Chapter 4.

Swaptions used in conjunction with callable bond issues may be used to the same effect as callable swaps. Of course, such a transaction will be cost-effective only if the bond market prices the embedded call more cheaply than the swap market. For example (see Figure 5.7), an issuer of a 10-year note callable in five years may transform the liability into a non-callable 10-year fixed-rate obligation by selling a receiver's swaption. If interest rates are higher in five years, the issuer will not call the bond, because it will cost more to refinance at the higher rates. Likewise, the buyer of the receiver's option will not exercise the right to receive at a rate below the current market rates. On the other hand, if interest rates are lower, the issuer will call the bonds in order to refinance at a lower rate, while the swaption buyer will exercise the option to receive the fixed rate in the swap. Thus, the

FIGURE 5.7   Transforming callable debt into non-callable debt using swaptions

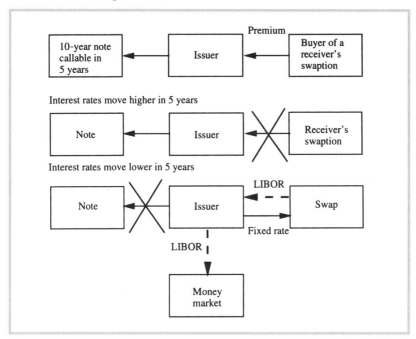

issuer will be left paying fixed on the swap for the remaining five years. The advantage of using this strategy is the issuer's cost of funding will be reduced by the option premium.

Alternatively, the issuer could sell a payer's swaption in conjunction with the 10-year bond issue callable in five years (see Figure 5.8). If interest rates are lower, the issuer will call the bond in order to refinance at a lower rate, but the buyer of the payer's option will not exercise the right to pay in the swap. If interest rates are higher in five years, the issuer will not call the bonds, but the buyer of the swaption will exercise the right to pay as the strike price is in-the-money. The issuer will be left a net floating-rate payer for the remaining five years, but the premium will be offset against the floating-rate payments producing sub-LIBOR funding. If interest rates drop in the remaining five years until the maturity of the bond, the issuer may still call the bond.

Swaptions may be used to create callable debt out of non-callable debt (see Figure 5.9). For example, the issuer of non-callable 10-year debt may offset the issue by buying a receiver's option maturing in five years. If interest rates rise in the future, then the issuer will not

FIGURE 5.8　Transforming fixed-rate callable debt into floating-rate debt using swaptions

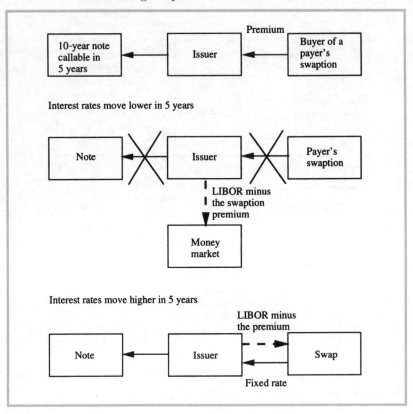

exercise the option. However, if interest rates decline, the issuer will exercise the option to receive in the swap. The fixed-rate payments on the swap will net off with the fixed-rate payments on the bond, and the issuer will be left paying a floating rate.

CAPS, FLOORS AND COLLARS

Caps

In order to help clarify the concept in relation to option theory, caps may be thought of as either calls or puts, depending on how they are viewed. A call is the right to buy, and one buys a call when the market

FIGURE 5.9 Transforming non-callable debt into callable debt using swaptions

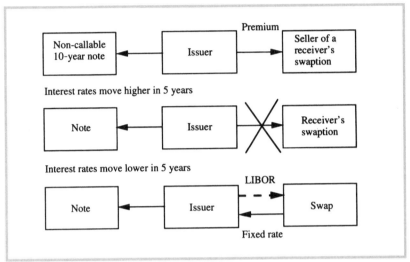

is expected to rise. A cap is a call in the respect that one would buy a cap when interest rates are expected to rise. On the other hand, one could also think of a cap as a put. One buys a put when the market is expected to fall. If bond theory were applied to the concept of the cap, as interest rates rise, the theoretical price would fall. Therefore, the cap may also be thought of as a put. A cap may also be thought of as a chain of European-style borrowers' options.

A cap's agreed strike price is an annualized rate based on three- or six-month LIBOR, starting on a specific date (often a forward start), and maturing on a specific date. From the start date to the maturity date, caps undergo multiple LIBOR rate fixings, yet the strike price remains the same until maturity. Typically, the principal amount on the cap remains the same throughout its life; however, where an amortizing funding/investment programme is involved, the capped principal amount may be tailored to match the amortizing schedule. Furthermore, once a cap is dealt, specialized documentation exists for cap transactions, and while some banks wish to provide their own documentation, most use documentation based on ISDA.

On each rollover date, the strike price is compared to the relevant LIBOR fixing. If LIBOR is the same as the strike price or lower than the strike price, no compensation is due. If LIBOR is above the strike price of the cap, then the writer of the cap must compensate the buyer for the difference. Payment is normally in arrears. Payment is calculated as:[5]

$$\text{LIBOR} - \text{strike price} \times \text{principal}$$
$$\times (\text{no. of days in the period}/360)$$

In exchange for insurance against an increase in interest rates, the buyer of a cap is required to pay an up-front premium quoted in flat basis points. While option pricing is beyond the scope of this book, the reader is encouraged to refer to the bibliography for further references.

A common user of a cap would be an institution looking to decrease the interest rate risk on a floating-rate liability such as a revolving credit agreement or a floating-rate note. Often, the treasurer will seek to match the term and the rollover dates on a funding programme with the rollover dates on the cap. For example, if an institution has a floating-rate funding programme lasting two years with a rollover cycle every six months, the treasurer may purchase a two-year cap against six-month LIBOR. The strike price of the cap will be set at the plain threshold, the level at which borrowing will become unprofitable.

An institution could fix its borrowing costs by entering into a swap, whereby the institution pays the fixed rate and receives the floating rate. On the settlement dates, the difference between the amount due by the fixed-rate payer and the amount due by the floating-rate payer would be payable by the counterparty owing the greater amount. If one were to think of the strike price on a cap as the fixed rate, a cap functions in the same way as a swap. However, the difference between the swap and the cap is that if the institution entered into the swap and interest rates fell, the institution may be liable for a net payment to the counterparty. On the other hand, if the institution bought a cap and interest rates fell, no payment would be due by the institution.

In other words, one advantage of a cap over a swap is that if rates increase, the firm will benefit from the hedge through compensation as the strike price moves in-the-money. At the same time, if rates do not rise, then all that is lost is the premium. Moreover, fixing borrowing costs with a cap may be quite inexpensive if the cap is bought at a time when volatility is low and if the cap is well out-of-the-money. The decision whether to enter into a cap or swap rests on the certainty of the premium versus the possibility that rates might move lower, thus providing the opportunity for lower funding costs in the future. Another advantage of a cap over a swap which should not be overlooked is that credit risk is only one way. The buyer of the cap assumes the credit risk of the seller of the cap.

Caps are often used by highly leveraged companies which still want to fix their cost of borrowing. They may also be used by debt issuers in less developed countries (LDCs). LDC debt issuers which often carry a weaker credit rating are forced to raise floating-rate funds at an unattractive rate. Furthermore, because of their weak credit standing, they are unable to participate in the swap market. While caps offer an alternative to the LDC borrower for fixing interest rate exposure, their usage of caps is limited, because they lack sufficient foreign exchange reserves.

Floors

A floor operates in the same way as a cap; however, its function is to lock in a lending rate, so a floor may be thought of as a chain of lenders' options. Floors are often used by floating-rate investors to protect themselves against an adverse decline in yields, thus guaranteeing a minimum yield from a floating-rate asset. For example, an investor holding a floating-rate note in a declining-rate environment may choose to buy a floor with a strike price set at the minimum acceptable level of return. If LIBOR is set below the strike price, then the buyer of the floor will be compensated by the writer for the difference between the strike price and LIBOR. Payment may be calculated as follows.[6]

$$\text{strike price} - \text{LIBOR} \times \text{principal}$$
$$\times \text{ (no. of days in the period/360)}$$

Collars

The combination of buying a cap and selling a floor is known as buying a collar. A treasurer may require a cap, yet the outright cost of the option may be prohibitive. By buying a cap and simultaneously selling a floor, the treasurer will be able to offset some of the cost of the cap with the premium from the floor. How much of the cost which is offset will depend on market conditions and the strike price of the cap and floor, because both of these elements are inherent in option pricing. Usually, the treasurer will endeavour to structure the collar so that both the cap and the floor are out-of-the-money, but the treasurer must aim to choose a cap and floor with strike prices which will yield the optimum net cost of the hedge.

For example, a treasurer may buy a cap at 13.00% and sell a floor at 10.00%. Therefore, the treasurer's borrowing cost is collared between 13.00 and 10.00%. Any time LIBOR is fixed at a rate over 13.00% on a roll over date, the firm will be compensated accordingly by the seller of the cap. On the other hand, if LIBOR is fixed at a rate below 10.00%, the firm must compensate the buyer of the floor. Normally, the notional principal on the cap and the floor will be equal to the funding liability being hedged. In other words, if the treasurer is hedging a $10 million liability, then the collar will be made up of a $10 million cap and a $10 million floor.

A lower net premium will be paid for a collar consisting of a floor with a strike price close to being at-the-money and a cap with a strike price which is deep out-of-the-money. It is possible to design the hedge so that it bears 'zero cost', but this may entail selling a floor which has a strike price very close to being at-the-money or even in-the-money, which in turn will pose more risk of the firm being required to make a payout if interest rates decline.

If the strike price and notional principal on cap and floor rates are equal, then this is essentially the same as paying the fixed rate on an interest rate swap which has a coupon rate equal to the strike price on the cap and the floor.[7] This is possible to envisage if one were to break down the transaction into its components. The buyer of a cap will acquire a position equivalent to the fixed-rate payer in a swap which has a coupon rate equal to the strike price. If rates move higher, then the buyer is compensated for the difference between LIBOR and the cap strike price, which is effectively the same as making a net payment as settlement for each period on a swap. The difference between the cap and the swap is that no payment is due if LIBOR is fixed at or below the cap strike price. However, when the buyer of a cap also sells a floor, payment will in fact be due if LIBOR is fixed at a rate below the floor strike price. The same would happen to the payer of the fixed rate in a swap if LIBOR were set below the swap coupon rate.

Alternatively, the treasurer may choose to enter into a participation agreement. Under this arrangement, the strike price of the floor and the strike price of the cap are equal, but the strike price of the floor is in-the-money and the strike price of the cap is out-of-the-money. Because the treasurer will be selling an in-the-money floor which will provide a higher premium, a lower notional principal is required on the floor in order to achieve the necessary cost reduction.[8] Therefore, whenever LIBOR is fixed at a rate higher than the strike price of the cap, the firm will be compensated by the writer of the total notional principal of the cap, and whenever LIBOR is fixed at a rate lower than the strike price of the floor, the firm will compensate the buyer of the floor, but only on a proportion of the notional principal of the cap. Thus, the firm participates in a lower funding cost whenever LIBOR is fixed at a rate less than the strike price of the cap.

In summary, if the treasurer feels rates *will* rise, then it is wise to enter into a swap as a payer of the fixed. If the treasurer feels that rates *may* rise, then a cap may be a more appropriate strategy. A floor may be purchased when rates may fall. A collar is beneficial when the view is that rates may rise, but the treasurer wishes to offset some of the premium. However, before doing anything it is wise to compare the benefit profiles of using each product whether it be swaps, caps, floors, collars or hybrids such as swaptions.

COMMODITY SWAPS

Innovations in the swap market have enabled users to link the transaction to various floating indices. Commodity swaps have proven to be such an innovation. Commodity swaps are similar interest rate swaps except the fixed and floating indices are based on a commodity, such as metals, fossil fuels or agricultural products. The swap also could involve current prices of a commodity against future spot prices, which enables users and producers to hedge future volatility. This structure is a useful hedging tool for manufacturers that require a certain commodity for the production of their goods, yet are exposed to an increase in the price of the commodity.

By and large, corporates that participate in the commodity derivatives market use the instruments to hedge against price volatility. Although the term 'hedge' conjures up a defensive type strategy, some corporates are much more proactive in the use of commodity derivatives.

Some companies use commodity swaps to lock in a commodity price below budget. For example, a company might plan to produce oil over a 10-year period, and the production profile for the field yields oil at $18 a barrel. If the company can lock in the production cost of $16 per barrel using a commodity swap, then a bank may be more likely to finance the project than if a hedge were not in place. Even at times when corporates with a high credit rating have access to relatively cheap funds, they can still use commodity swaps to lower their cost of funding further without increasing their risk.

The commodity swaps market is still dwarfed by the interest rate and currency swap market. Yet, commodity swaps are becoming more commonplace and more widely accepted. But critics say that the market suffers from a lack of communication between banks and corporates, and this hinders the market's growth. Since many bankers do not understand the underlying commodity and the market practices, they are not in a position to put ideas forward to corporates.

SUMMARY

One of the simplest forms of interest rate swaps is the basis swap. LIBOR-LIBOR basis swaps may be used to solve a mismatch in a portfolio or as a means of speculating on interest rate differentials. Prime-LIBOR basis swaps may be used to fund LIBOR priced assets on a Prime rate basis and Prime priced assets on the basis of LIBOR. CP-LIBOR swaps may be used by companies wishing to simulate the US commercial paper market without having to comply with the requirements of a commercial paper programme.

In an amortizing swap, the principal reduces at a fixed amount periodically throughout the life of the swap. The roller-coaster swap is a variation on the amortizing swap, and in this structure, the principal increases and decreases over the life of the swap. Amortizing swaps and roller-coaster swaps are ideal for companies involved in projects with loan accounts attached. Mortgages and leasing agreements may also be matched with these swap structures.

LIBOR adjustments and off-market coupon swaps may be used in conjunction with a new issue or a firm's existing borrowings. LIBOR-in-arrears swaps are those which have the LIBOR fixing at the end of the payment period rather than at the beginning of the payment period. This structure may be used when the swap user expects that short-term rates will remain stable or decrease. Participation swaps perform as a cap on the full notional principal if LIBOR is set above the agreed interest rate, and perform as a swap on a portion of the notional principal if LIBOR is set below the agreed interest rate. Zero-coupon swaps may be used in conjunction with zero-coupon bonds.

Option products have been developed to complement the swap market. A user may buy or sell a swaption, which is an option on a swap. The user may buy the right to pay the fixed rate, sell the right to pay the fixed rate, buy the right to receive the fixed rate or sell the right to receive the fixed rate. Like other options, the swaption will have a strike price which if exercised will serve as the fixed rate on the swap. Swaptions may be swap settled or cash settled, and may be dealt American-style or European-style, but most common swaptions are dealt European-style with a cash settlement.

Caps, floors and collars are also effective option products used for risk management. The buyer of a cap will be compensated if LIBOR is fixed above the strike price, and the buyer of a floor will be compensated if LIBOR is fixed below the strike price. If one simultaneously buys a cap and sells a floor, this is known as a collar, because the borrowing cost will be collared between the two strike prices. One of the main advantages of the collar is that the user is able to offset some of the cost of buying a cap with the premium gained from selling the floor.

Although they are not as prevalent as interest rate and currency swaps, the commodity swap is gaining acceptance. This structure allows the user to link the cost of borrowing to the price of a specific commodity.

Notes

1. A/360 means 'the actual number of days/360'.
2. The bank may adjust this figure by approximately 0.13 to 0.25% to allow for its own profit margin.
3. Because the replacement cost will automatically be greater at the inception of the swap, this structure will carry a higher credit risk. This is discussed in more detail in Chapter 6.
4. This example assumes no amortization and the borrower can fund at LIBOR flat.
5. A 365-day count basis is used in calculating sterling caps.
6. A 365-day count basis is used in calculating sterling floors.
7. If the strike price is above the current market level, then this is equivalent to establishing a swap with an off-market coupon.
8. The notional principal can be calculated using a ratio of the cap and floor prices.

Bibliography

Antl, Boris (ed.) (1986). *Swap Finance, Vols I and II*. London: Euromoney Publications Ltd.

Brown, Keith C. and Smith, Donald J. (1988). 'Recent innovations in interest rate risk management and the reintermediation of commercial banking', *Financial Management*, vol. 17, winter, pp. 45–58.

Das, Satyajit (1989). *Swap Financing*. London: IFR Publishing Ltd.

DeCovny, Sherree (1993). 'From the ground up', *Finance & Treasury*, 13 September, p. 6.

DeCovny, Sherree and Tacchi, Christine (1991). *Hedging Strategies*. Cambridge: Woodhead-Faulkner (Publishers) Ltd.

Folkerts-Landau, David (1989). 'Management of interest rate risk by LDCs', *Finance and Development*, vol. 26, June, pp. 20–3.

Henderson, Schuyler K. and Price, John A. M. (1988). *Currency and Interest Rate Swaps*, 2nd edition. London: Butterworths.

Ireland, Louise (1988). 'Getting a fix with swaps', *Corporate Finance*, no. 47, October, pp. 39, 42.

May, Michael (1990). 'To swap or not to swap', *The Treasurer*, vol. 12, no. 2, February, pp. 14–20.

Smith, Donald (1987). 'Putting the cap on options', *Corporate Finance*, January, pp. 20–2.

Smith Jr., Clifford W., Smithson, Charles W. and Macdonald
    Wakeman, Lee (1986). 'The evolving market for swaps', *Midland
    Corporate Finance Journal*, winter, pp. 20–32.

LEGAL AND ACCOUNTING CONSIDERATIONS

6

The majority of this book has focused on the technical side of trading swaps; however, the swap does not end when the deal is closed. Credit risk must be monitored, documentation must be negotiated and signed, and the swap must be incorporated into the firm's accounts. Moreover, personnel must ensure the swap complies with the regulations set forth by the authorities. Just as the swap trader must make every effort to price a swap correctly so as not to make a loss, the personnel who deal with the swap in the post-transaction phase must do exactly the same.

COUNTERPARTY RISK AND ASSESSING CREDIT EXPOSURE

Credit risk plays an extremely important role in the pricing of swaps. Theoretically an interest swap bears less counterparty risk than a loan, because the principal of a loan is 'nominal' – that is, it is actually exchanged. In an interest rate swap, the principal is 'notional' – that is, it is not exchanged, but is used only as a base for interest rate calculations. However, this is not the case with currency swaps where there is an actual exchange of principal.

When a firm raises funds in the capital markets, it automatically becomes a debtor. However, once the firm enters into a swap against the liability, it becomes a debtor twice and a creditor. An important consideration is that the firm will be using up its credit lines, and thus the treasurer should ensure that this opportunity cost is taken into consideration prior to entering into the swap transaction. In the worst case, future projects may be jeopardized because of limited credit lines.

From the bank's point of view, the reason why the counterparty is entering into the swap should have a bearing on the credit risk weighting. If the purpose of the swap is to hedge financial exposure, then the probability of the firm defaulting will be considerably lower, thus a lower risk premium can be built into the swap price. On the other hand, if the counterparty is entering into the swap for speculative purposes, the risk of default will be greater, and the price of the swap will reflect a higher risk premium.

When the focus is placed on the company as a whole rather than one transaction, this is known as 'enterprise risk'. Enterprise risk can have an effect on credit risk. To illustrate, consider the case of Sears Roebuck and Company and their accounts from 31 December 1984. One analyst commented that by managing the firm's debt exposure through the swap market:

> *Sears had effectively increased its percentage of fixed-rate debt to 50% of total borrowings and that a 1% swing, up or down, in market interest rates now meant a $0.06 change in Sear's earnings per share (EPS), in contrast to a $0.12 effect on EPS before completion of the swaps.*[1]

Credit risk can be assessed by looking at the replacement cost of the swap if the counterparty defaults. For example, if a firm is paying the fixed rate in the swap, and the counterparty defaults at a time when interest rates are higher than the fixed rate, the firm will suffer a loss. Of course, if the counterparty defaults at a time when rates are lower, the bankrupt counterparty or trustee will more than likely honour the payments under the swap, because it is in-the-money. The credit exposure on the swap will be the loss or gain equal to the present value of the annuity represented by the difference between the original coupon on the swap and the current market rate for the maturity multiplied by the notional principal. Providing the market does not move, the credit risk on a swap when it is first transacted is zero.

It is suggested that there are seven items which should be considered in assessing default risk for an interest rate swap: the credit rating of the contracting firm, the correlation between the contracting firm's value and interest rates, the volatility of interest rates, the slope of the term structure, the maturity of the swap, the frequency of the difference checks, and whether some form of performance bond is posted.[2] Some banks calculate credit risk using option-based delta techniques.

CENTRAL BANK/GOVERNMENTAL REGULATION AND BIS CAPITAL REQUIREMENTS

With the growth of the swap market, the various regulatory authorities have become concerned over the level of risk assumed by banks and other swap counterparties. In January 1987, the US regulatory authorities including the Federal Reserve Bank, the Office of the Comptroller of the Currency and the Federal Deposit Insurance Corporation together with the Bank of England issued a joint proposal for capital adequacy requirements, leading the way for other monetary authorities in Japan, Germany and Canada. In a joint report by the Federal Reserve Bank and the Bank of England, it was stated: 'The credit risks inherent in such contracts now constitute a significant element of the risk profiles of some banking organizations, notably the large multinational banking organizations that act as intermediaries between end-users of these contracts.'[3] In December 1987, the Basle Committee on Banking Regulations and Supervisory Practices of the Bank for International Settlements (BIS) proposed to increase the capital requirements for institutions involved in the swap markets. BIS issued the statement that 'gross income from the transaction is insufficient, on average, to compensate fully for their inherent risks.'[4]

One of the most important items in the BIS proposal was to establish the measurement of capital and capital requirements in relation to risk profiles. In order to do this, the BIS set out five risk categories with weights of 0, 10, 20, 50 and 100%. The BIS put forward the following recommendations in the assignment of claims which were subject to a national regulatory authority's discretion. These did not take into account either the individual credit standing of the counterparty or guarantees by any authority other than domestic public sector institutions.[5]

CATEGORY	RECOMMENDATION
0, 20%	Claims on multinational lending and regional development institutions.
20%	Claims on domestic banks and foreign banks with a maturity of one year or less. Local currency claims on foreign governments financed by local currency liabilities.

0, 10, 20%	Claims on or guaranteed by domestic central governments. Claims collateralized by cash or by domestic central securities.
0, 10, 20, 50%	Claims on or guaranteed by or collateralized by the securities of other domestic public sector entities. Claims related to swaps and other interest rate and foreign exchange rate instruments.
100%	Claims on private entities and individuals. Long-term claims on foreign banks. Claims on foreign governments that involve transfer risk. All other assets.

The US regulatory authorities issued a draft notice in January 1988 establishing their own categories as follows:

0%	Claims with a maturity of 90 days or less.
10%	Claims on or guaranteed by or collateralized by the securities of the US government or governmental agencies backed by the US government
20%	Claims on or guaranteed by or collateralized by the securities of the US government-sponsored agencies and US state and local governments. Claims on multinational lending and regional development institutions in which the US is a member or shareholder.
50%	Claims on special purpose revenue bonds.

The Bank of England set out its own categories in January 1988 which do not include a category for claims collateralized by government securities, as follows:

10%	UK institutions' claims on or guaranteed by the UK government with maturities less than one year.
20%	Other claims on or guaranteed by the UK government and all claims on or guaranteed by local authorities and other public sector bodies. Claims on multinational institutions.

The BIS proposal provided for a five-year transition period. By January 1991, all banks were required to have capital equal to 7.25% of their assets. By 1992 this was increased to 8%. National regulatory authorities are within their rights to impose stricter requirements as they see fit. For example, the Federal Reserve uses another measure known as the 'tangible common equity ratio' which must equal 4% of banks' total assets. While the larger banks in the US and the UK have no trouble meeting these requirements, they are now coming under pressure as more capital is having to be set aside for bad debts, particularly on non-performing property loans.

In order to establish a risk category for claims the credit equivalent amount must be calculated which is equal to the potential exposure (made up of the notional principal × a conversion factor) plus the current exposure (the replacement cost). The conversion factors used to determine the potential exposure are based on a statistical model which takes into account the potential volatility of interest rates and exchange rates and the implications of movements in rates for replacement costs of various contracts. The problem with this method is that the same conversion factor is used for all currency swaps, regardless of the currency or swap maturity. As some currencies are more volatile than others, and swaps with longer maturities tend to be more volatile, the accuracy of the conversion factors is questionable. Moreover, the equation does not take into account whether the swaps have been entered into for hedging or speculative purposes.[6]

The amount of capital which must be set aside to support a portfolio is the total of the credit equivalent amounts multiplied by 50% and again by the capital adequacy requirement which is currently 7.25%. For example, if a bank has entered into swap transactions with a counterparty and the sum total of the credit equivalent amounts from each of the transactions is $5,000,000 then the bank would have to set aside $181,250 in capital, being $5,000,000 × 50% × 7.25%.

One consideration was how exposure should be calculated. For example, are two offsetting swaps to be counted as two swaps or as a flat position? The original BIS proposal did not permit netting. The argument behind counting the offsetting swaps as two open positions is focused on the possibility that if one counterparty defaults, the bank is exposed to an amount equal to the replacement cost. Another consideration was there is no way to protect against spread risk. Regardless, the regulatory authorities are concerned that institutions which run large swap portfolios should have a specified amount of capital against the exposure on the swap portfolio.

The greatest impact of capital adequacy requirements on the swap market is on very complex, multi-leg transactions, because when all of the various costs and risks are taken into account, the bank's profit margins may be substantially reduced. In addition, it is argued that the regulations put banks at a disadvantage in relation to competitors which are not subject to capital adequacy requirements. Finally, banks which were previously willing to enter into currency swap transactions are now less willing to do so, and this has had a negative impact on the liquidity of the currency swap market.

LEGAL QUESTIONS AND EXAMPLES OF SWAP DEFAULTS

Between 1980 and 1988, approximately $1 trillion in swaps were transacted. Of these, there were 22 swap defaults with recorded losses totalling $32 million.[7] In order to qualify as a default, the swap contract must have negative value, and the counterparty must be in bankruptcy. Some institutions have taken action to prevent potential disasters. For example, the World Bank arranged a swap insurance programme with Aetna Casualty and Surety Company which operates in a similar way to personal mortgage insurance. The World Bank assumes the interest rate risk while Aetna assumes the default risk. This arrangement is extremely beneficial to the World Bank, because it has a policy not to deal with institutions with a credit rating below AA. Yet, the possibility of default and legal risk has been a focal point of the swap market for the last several years, highlighted by a number of cases in which entities incurred losses from swaps and other derivatives.

The UK local authority debacle

In this case, the legality of off-balance sheet transactions undertaken by 77 local authorities, in particular the London Borough of Hammersmith and Fulham, was brought into question. UK local authorities were almost natural users of the swap. They had an advantage over most borrowers in that they had access to the Public Works Loans Board (PWLB) where they could borrow floating-rate funds with the option to convert into fixed-rate funds on every rollover date at interest rates almost as advantageous as those obtained by the government in the gilt-edged market. Therefore, they could effectively borrow cheap fixed-rate funds and later swap them into floating-rate liabilities. This became a popular strategy at the time when local authority treasurers held the view that interest rates would decline. At the same time, the government's war on local authorities included a strong possibility of rate capping. So local authority treasurers were under pressure to produce creative solutions to their potential shortfall of cash.

Hammersmith and Fulham entered into approximately 600 transactions including swaps, swaptions and gilt options having a total notional principal amount of about £6 billion. By the end of March 1989, many of the deals had matured or been offset, but the Council still had on its books 295 deals with a notional principal of approximately £3 billion.

This is compared to the Council's underlying borrowings of £350–390 million. The deals were structured so that the Council would make a profit if interest rates declined. Unfortunately, toward the end of 1988, interest rates started to climb, thus throwing Hammersmith and Fulham's positions into a loss of around £160 million.

The legal decision on the case hinged on the question of whether Hammersmith and Fulham's trades were *intra vires* (undertaken as part of the proper management of the Council's funds under Section 111 of the Local Government Finance Act of 1982) or *ultra vires* (transacted for trading purposes). More specifically, the court decision was to be based on whether the deals were capable of being within the powers of the local authority, whether the transactions were entered into in good faith as a proper exercise of those powers, and whether the deals were properly authorized, recorded and maintained in the internal accounts.

The court ruled the swaps were *ultra vires*, and the banks appealed in what evolved into a protracted legal battle. The court's decision was upheld by the Appeal Court in January 1991.

Since then, there have been several other notable cases in the US where swaps and other derivatives have been blamed for losses. The government of Orange County, California suffered substantial losses in the mid-1990s from its derivatives dealings in a case strikingly similar to the UK local authorities. In the corporate world, Proctor & Gamble took a $157 million pre-tax charge and Air Products & Chemicals took a $60 million pre-tax charge arising from losses on interest rate swaps. In addition, Gibson Greetings sued Bankers Trust for being misled about the risks of swaps.

The number and financial magnitude of these cases has led to a rash of studies about the risks and the need for regulation of derivatives, including swaps. Studies have been conducted by several organizations, including the BIS, the G10, and the General Accounting Office in the US.

DOCUMENTATION

In the mid-1980s, swap market participants realized that the standardization of swap documentation would give a boost to the market, because it would reduce the potential for future disagreements, save time and money, and facilitate the development of the secondary market. In response to the demand, the International Swap Dealers Association (ISDA) issued a code of Standard Wording, Assumptions and Provisions for Swaps (the ISDA swap code) in 1985. This was updated in 1987 when ISDA published two standard agreements: Interest Rate Swap Agreement and Interest Rate and Currency Exchange Agreement, both of which can be found in Appendix 2. These agreements are updated periodically by ISDA. An up-to-date list of documentation available can be found in Appendix 3.

ISDA documentation is now the most widely used format in the swap market, and active swap market participants often negotiate master agreements based on ISDA. Other less widely used documentation formats exist including British Bankers Association's Interest Rate Swaps (BBAIRS) and Australian Financial Markets Association's General Terms and Conditions for Australian Dollar Fixed and Floating Interest Rate Swaps (AIRS Terms.) The reason BBAIRS terms are less frequently used is because the documentation only covers swaps with maturities up to two years, although there is an extended BBAIRS format. AIRS Terms, of course, have a limited application to Australian dollar swaps.

Despite its acceptance, many swap users have criticized ISDA documentation on the basis that it is too complex. Since ISDA members are banks, it is not geared toward large corporates who use swaps and should have master documentation in place.

Many corporates accept, with little or no negotiation, ISDA documentation submitted by their counterparties. Too frequently, a firm finds out further down the road that the terms of the swap agreement are much more restrictive on the corporation than are the covenants on the transaction being hedged. In addition, many corporates are bound by varying restrictions on their swap agreements for lack of uniform policies on certain key credit issues. Some end users either do not link the documentation process or they become intimidated by it.

The standard ISDA documentation contains provisions for payment obligations and mechanics, yield protection, representations and warranties, covenants usually applying to both parties, termination events which will affect the right or obligation to cancel the swap, events of default, consequences of default, indemnity and liquidated damages provisions, and miscellaneous provisions including contractual currency, notice, governing law and assignability. The schedule to the ISDA agreement contains several optional provisions that parties may select, providing the counterparties with a degree of flexibility. While the ISDA agreement is designed for use under New York or English law, there are some instances where the provisions of the local law of the party's jurisdiction of incorporation will prevail, for example, in the event of bankruptcy or insolvency.

Payment provisions

Payment provisions refer to the exact payment dates, non-business day conventions, and interest payment calculations. The exact payment dates will be specified as the rollover dates on the fixed and floating side of the swap. A non-business day is a day which banks are not open in a particular centre. If banks are closed, then payments cannot be made or received. Normally, if the rollover date falls on a Sunday or a holiday, the payment will be made the succeeding good business day, except at the end of a month in which case the payment would be made on the preceding good business day. The documentation will also stipulate the method of calculating the floating-rate interest payments. Depending on the currency, the floating rate is posted on Telerate. Non-payment would constitute a breach of contract, and the payee would be able to claim damages.

Tax indemnities

Under the ISDA agreement, counterparties are required to make payments free of deduction or withholding taxes; however, an 'affected party' – that is, one that is required to 'gross up' swap payments subject to withholding tax – is allowed to terminate affected transactions on a 'no fault' basis. The ISDA agreement spells out when the counterparty is obligated and when it is not obligated to 'gross up' in the event of an 'indemnifiable tax' – for example, if there is a change in the tax law including a change in a treaty or regulation or in its interpretation of application.

Swap payments are generally regarded as constituting 'business profits' rather than 'interest'. The ISDA agreement avoids using the word 'interest', because various countries have a statutory rate of withholding tax on interest payment, although certain US and European country treaties reduce the rate of withholding on interest payments to zero. If swap payments were to be considered 'interest' then this would constitute a 'change in the tax law' and there would be an obligation to gross up, regardless of the payee tax representations.

Representations and covenants

Once both counterparties in a swap transaction sign the documentation, the ISDA agreement is recognized as legal, valid, binding and enforceable. Both counterparties agree that they have the power to execute and perform the agreement with all of the necessary consents in place, and that the agreement is not in conflict with either the law or with other documents. Moreover, each party agrees to maintain and obtain in the future all necessary consents and to comply with all applicable material laws. Documents specified in the Schedule or any confirmation shall be provided by the specified date.

Through the agreement, each party declares an absence of any event of default or termination event and an absence of any material litigation. The counterparties guarantee the accuracy of any written information provided by a party and any tax representation of a party specified in the Schedule. The counterparties agree to give notice upon becoming aware that any payee tax representation is untrue, and each party agrees to pay any stamp tax imposed by the jurisdiction in which it is located.

Events of default

An event of default would occur in any of the following circumstances:

1. Failure to pay any amount due within three business days after notice of such failure is given to a party.

2. Failure to perform any other obligation under the agreement within 30 days of notice.

3. A representation, other than a tax representation, which relieves only the non-defaulting party in certain circumstances of its obligation to gross up proving to be untrue.

4. Default under and termination of any specified swap (as such term is defined by the parties in the Schedule) of a party.

5. Bankruptcy, insolvency, dissolution or liquidation of a party.

6. Merger of a party without its successor entity assuming the obligations of the party under the agreement.

Termination events

A termination event is an event which occurs that makes it illegal for a party, or a specified entity of a party, to make any payment due or to perform any other material obligation under the agreement. If an indemnifiable tax has been imposed, if there is a substantial likelihood that an indemnifiable tax will be imposed on the next payment date, or if an indemnifiable tax will be imposed as a result of a merger, known as a tax event upon merger, this would qualify as a termination event. A credit event upon merger would also qualify as a termination event. This means that if one of the swap counterparties merges with an entity which is a materially weaker credit, and the merger damages the credit standing of the swap counterparty, then this would constitute a termination event.

Under the ISDA agreement, once a party defaults, the non-defaulting party can specify an early termination date for all outstanding swaps. The termination date has to be within 20 days of the notice to the defaulting party, except in the case of bankruptcy or insolvency where the termination date will be on a date immediately preceding the bankruptcy.

The affected party is required to give notice to the other party. An affected party is the party which cannot perform because of an illegality, the party that must gross up because of a tax event or the surviving entity of a party in the case of a tax event upon merger or a credit event upon merger. In the case of a tax event, the affected party should try to eliminate the event by transferring its obligations within 30 days to a branch, office or affiliate in another jurisdiction in such a manner that would not cause a material loss. If this cannot be done, either party can set an early termination date within 20 days of notice for all outstanding swaps.

Some swap counterparties slightly vary the terms of termination events. For example, some parties request that a change in majority ownership of a party qualifies as an event of default. Others request a reduction in the 30-day period within which a party must use reasonable efforts to transfer its obligations upon the occurrence of a tax event. Insolvency as an event of default is occasionally eliminated, because it is often unclear when a party may be legally deemed insolvent. However, even though it might be eliminated as an event of default, under the agreement it does not eliminate the right of the other party to take action relating to insolvency, bankruptcy, dissolution or liquidation. Some counterparties also eliminate the substantial likelihood of the imposition of an indemnifiable tax as a termination event.

In order to calculate the non-defaulting party's gain or loss as compensation on termination, the following method is usually employed. The parties may obtain quotes from four leading market-makers for each outstanding swap to replace the remaining payments due. The quote is the average of the four disregarding the highest and lowest quote. If for some reason only three quotes are obtained, the middle quote may be used as the settlement price.

Other provisions

Assignment Under the ISDA agreement, a counterparty may assign a swap, but only after obtaining the permission of the original swap counterparty.

Contractual currency The swap counterparties agree to make any payments in a specified currency, but if there is a shortfall due to foreign exchange loss, then the payer has to indemnify the payee for the loss.

Multibranch parties Payments can be made or received from any of the party's branches, but one branch must be specified from the outset, and the branch cannot be changed without written consent from the counterparty.

Notices Notices may be given by hand, overnight courier, telex, certified or registered mail or fax.

Jurisdiction The swap counterparties can choose to have the swap contract governed under English law or New York law. Foreigners can elect to have New York law, provided that the amount at stake is above a minimum threshold, but US federal courts may not have subject-matter jurisdiction over a dispute between two foreign parties.

Waiver of immunities Each party waives to the fullest extent possible all immunity on grounds of sovereignty or other similar grounds. Under the Foreign Sovereign Immunities Act 1976 (US) a federal court may have jurisdiction over a suit by a foreign plaintiff against a foreign defendant if the defendant raises sovereign immunity as a defence.

SWAPS ACCOUNTING

The process toward greater standardization of swaps contracts has led to more standardization in accounting procedures. Accountants tend to break swap transactions into four categories: matched swaps, hedged swaps, unmatched swaps and offsetting swaps. A matched swap is one which is dealt against an existing asset or liability. A hedged swap is one which has a bond or futures transaction against it which will reduce interest rate exposure. An unmatched swap is one which is

entered into for speculative purposes and does not have a corresponding asset, liability, bond or futures contract against it. At offsetting
swap is used mainly by financial intermediaries, and is transacted
against an opposing swap position.

The next two sections will examine the accounting conventions
used in two major swap centres: the United Kingdom and the United
States.

Swaps accounting practices in the United Kingdom

Statements of Standard Accounting Practice (SSAPs) In swaps
accounting, the rules set forth in SSAP 2 – Disclosure of Accounting
Policies; SSAP 18 – Accounting for Contingencies; and SSAP 20 –
Foreign Currency Translation are often used. The SSAPs are also
supported by the 1989 Companies Act as well as the proposed
Statement of Recommended Practice (SORP) on accounting for off-
balance sheet transactions which is to be issued by the British Bankers
Association.

SSAP 2 deals with the accruals concept of matching the profits on
the swap against the related loan interest payments; therefore, it
automatically implies that there must be matching underlying debt
against the swap transaction, making the swap a hedging instrument
rather than a trading instrument:

> The 'accruals' concept; revenue and cost are accrued (that is,
> recognized as they are earned or incurred, not as money is
> received or paid), matched with one another so far as their
> relationship can be established or justifiably assumed, and dealt
> with in the profit and loss account of the period to which they
> relate; provided that where the accruals concept is consistent
> with the 'prudence' concept, the latter prevails. The accruals
> concept implies that the profit and loss account reflects changes
> in the amount of net assets that arise out of the transactions of
> the relevant period (other than distributions or subscriptions of
> capital and unrealized surpluses arising on revaluation of fixed
> assets). Revenue and profits dealt with in the profit and loss
> account are matched and associated costs and expenses by
> including in the same account the cost incurred in earning them
> (so far as these are material and identifiable).[8]

SSAP 18 – Accounting for Contingencies provides guidelines for
dealing with contingent gains or losses in financial statements:

> The treatment of a contingency existing at the balance sheet
> date is determined by its expected outcome. In addition to

accruals under the fundamental concept of prudence in SSAP 2 – Disclosure of Accounting Policies, more contingent losses will be accrued in financial statements where it is probable that a future event will confirm a loss which can be estimated with reasonable accuracy at the date on which the financial statements are approved by the board of directors.[9]

In respect of each contingency which is required to be disclosed . . . the following information should be stated by way of notes in financial statements:

a. *the nature of the contingency;*

b. *the uncertainties which are expected to affect the ultimate outcome; and*

c. *a prudent estimate of the financial effect made at the date on which the financial statements are approved by the board of directors, or a statement that it is not practicable to make such an estimate.*[10]

SSAP 20 – Foreign Currency Translation sets out a standard accounting practice for foreign currency translation, but does not set out standards for calculating foreign exchange gains or losses which arise out of a firm's normal currency dealing operations. Firms which enter into business transactions denominated in foreign currencies are required to translate the foreign currency into the firm's normal reporting currency on financial statements:

The result of each transaction should normally be translated into the company's local currency using the exchange rate in operation on the date on which the transaction occurred; however, if the rates do not fluctuate significantly, an average rate for a period may be used as an approximation. Where the transaction is to be settled at a contracted rate, that rate should be used; where a trading transaction is covered by a related or matching forward contract, the rate of exchange specified in that contract may be used.[11]

Under the guidelines of the closing rate/net investment method in SSAP 20, in the case of a subsidiary company for consolidation purposes it is permissible to use the closing rate or an average rate for the accounting period for the purposes of translation of foreign currencies. However, it is recommended that the same method be used from period to period.

Accounting for intermediaries, financial institutions and corporate users With the guidelines from the SSAPs in mind, accounting for swaps will depend on the use of the swap and the type of user. For UK financial institutions, the view is that swaps should be marked-to-market by discounting the known fixed future cash flows using net present value calculations. Since LIBOR is usually fixed at the beginning of the period and settled in arrears, it is also acceptable to take the floating cash flows which are already known into account when calculating the net present value. The interest rate used to discount the cash flows can either be the zero-coupon rates or the current swap rate for the maturity.

From the accountant's point of view, when a swap is traded a bank must take into consideration its exposure or costs which may arise over the life of the swap. These costs must be taken into account by a reduction in the amount of profit taken. Two major elements must be considered: replacement cost and capital cost. When a bank has a swap on its books which is matched, the bank is exposed to the possibility that the counterparty may default by a failure to make payments. If this happens, the bank would be left with an open position which may result in a profit or a loss. This is known as the replacement cost.

Although the deferral of income to represent the replacement cost can be calculated in a number of ways, the following method is one which may be employed:[12]

$$NP \times n \times CS \times V\%$$

where: NP = notional principal; n = number of years; CS = commercial spread applicable to the counterparty risk; and $V\%$ = expected annual percentage change in interest rates.

The Basle Convergence rules state that a minimum of capital representing 8% of risk assets must be maintained. This cost of capital may be accounted for by deferring an element of the up-front present value profit, thus spreading a constant return on the capital allocated over the life of the swap.

A corporate user of interest rate swaps is likely to have entered into the transaction for the purpose of lowering the firm's overall cost of funding. Therefore, when the accounts of the firm are being drawn up, the funding rate reflected in the accounts should be adjusted taking into consideration both the actual rate of borrowing plus the net payment or receipt from the interest rate swap. The payments and receipts should be evenly accrued over the period to which the cash flow relates. The interest cost of the firm's borrowings as explained above should be accrued on a straight line basis over the relevant rollover periods and should be charged to the profit and loss account.

If the swap is a currency swap and there is a front-to-back exchange of principal, then the initial exchange will appear on the balance sheet as a currency position. This is balanced by an equal and offsetting currency position at the same initial spot rate off-balance sheet to account for the re-exchange of principal at maturity. In order to avoid the transaction being improperly reflected on the profit and loss account, both the exchange on inception of the swap and the re-exchange at maturity should be revalued at closing spot rates of exchange. However, this may not be the case if the foreign currency funds are going to be invested in an overseas subsidiary and carried at historical exchange rates. In this event, it may be more appropriate not to revalue the initial exchange of principal on the balance sheet, but instead to carry it at the original exchange rate. The net cash flow occurring under the swap on each rollover is accrued evenly over the period to which the cash flow relates. Like accounting for interest rate swaps, the periodic payments on currency swaps should be treated as an adjustment to interest expense.

Taxation

When a firm is considering the tax implications of dealing in swaps, several elements must be taken into consideration including the characterization of the payments and receipts and the time they are included in the computation of income subject to tax. The firm must also decide whether revaluations for financial reporting purposes result in a taxable event and whether exchange gains or losses should be brought into the tax computation. Finally, the firm must carefully consider international tax issues, and in particular investigations must be made into whether double tax treaties are in place.

A couple of points are worth noting with regard to the taxation of swaps accounting in the United Kingdom. First, under section 77, Taxes Act 1988 there is a provision to allow a deduction for costs of arranging qualifying loan finance. Swap arrangement fees may be tax deductible in computing trading profits where it is paid by a bank or financial institution. However, for other firms the issue of whether the fees are tax deductible is not as clear cut. Second, while interest payments on borrowings are tax deductible, UK tax law does not recognize swap payments as 'interest' payments, because the principal is notional.

The UK Inland Revenue has established the following guidelines for the tax treatment of swaps:[13]

1. Swap payments by or to a recognized UK banking business (where it acts as principal and not agent) can be made gross without any withholding on the bank or the UK non-bank payer.

For these purposes a 'recognized UK banking business' is one approved by the Revenue under Section 349(3), Taxes Act 1988 and so could include the UK branch of an overseas bank.[14]

2. Such UK banking business will, in most cases, be able to deduct such swap payments and be taxable on receipts of its normal banking activities.

3. A UK trading company can treat such swap payments as a normal trading expense.

4. A UK investment company can deduct such swap payments on a cash payments basis under Section 338, Taxes Act 1988.

5. Receipts of swap payments by a non-banking business will be taxed as investment income where there is either a UK counterparty (Schedule D-III) or a non-UK counterparty (Schedule D-IV).

In the event a swap has been cancelled or terminated, any receipt or payment of fees may be treated as taxable profit or loss. In the case of an assignment, if a replacement counterparty has made or received a payment as a fee for taking over the swap, then that payment may be tied to the swap contract and thus amortized over the life of the contract. As a result, assignments are often more effective than cancellations, unless the swap is attached to an underlying asset or liability which has also been cancelled, in which case this is irrelevant.

Non-UK resident counterparties should be sure that a double tax treaty exists between the United Kingdom and the home country to ensure there will be no withholding of UK tax. In addition, if two UK corporates deal a swap directly, then the payments will be eligible for withholding tax.

One taxation issue which has yet to be resolved occurs when a non-bank counterparty has entered into a currency swap. The firm must distinguish its foreign exchange gains and losses between capital assets (taxed as capital gains) and liabilities which are outside the scope of UK law. While a detailed discussion of this issue is beyond the scope of this book, readers can refer to three cases as a reference: Marine Midland, FW Woolworth plc v. Beauchamp, and Overseas Containers (Finance) Ltd. v. Stokes.

Swaps accounting practices in the United States

At the time of writing there is no specific accounting pronouncement in the United States which covers interest rate swaps. However, the

Financial Accounting Standards Board has issued an Exposure Draft addressing the accounting for derivative instruments and the derivative portion of certain other contracts that have similar characteristics and for hedging activities.

Prior to this statement, FAS Statement no. 80, Accounting for Futures Contracts, was used to shed some light on accounting for hedges. According to Statement no. 80, how a firm accounts for futures contracts depends upon the purpose for which the contracts were bought or sold. Futures positions are marked-to-market unless they qualify as a hedge for an existing or anticipated asset or liability, and the firm must be able to show a match between a futures position and an existing or anticipated asset, liability or commitment. If a futures position is put on as a hedge, the change in its current market value is reported as an adjustment to the carrying value of the underlying instrument unless the instrument is carried at fair value, in which case the change in the market value of futures is reported in income. If a futures position is put on to hedge an anticipated transaction, then the cumulative change in the market value of the futures contract is accounted for once the transaction actually occurs.

FAS 52 specifically covers currency swaps. Under the guidelines, currency swaps are treated as foreign exchange transactions and are valued according to the reason for entering into the transaction. FAS 52 mentions four methods of valuation. First, if the purpose of the transaction is to hedge a net investment in a foreign subsidiary or affiliate, then an adjustment for gains or losses is to be made to shareholders' equity. Second, if the purpose of the transaction is to hedge a foreign currency position or foreign currency debt, then gains or losses are to be reported in net income. Third, if the purpose is to hedge a foreign currency commitment, for example, interest payments on foreign currency debt, then gains or losses are deferred and included in the measurement of the foreign currency transaction. Finally, if the firm enters into a currency swap purely for speculative purposes, then gains or losses must be reported in net income. 16 FAS 52 requires the use of the average rate for the translation of a subsidiary company's profit and loss account.

Accounting for intermediaries, financial institutions and corporate users

If the financial intermediary is acting solely as an agent in a matched swap, the only gain to the intermediary will be a fee. Depending on the firm's accounting policy over a period of time, the fee could be recorded in income immediately following the transaction, or any net fees paid or received under a matched or hedged swap agreement should be deferred and amortized to income or interest expense over the life of the swap. If the fee will not be paid up-front, then the fee may be recorded as the discounted present value of the amount to be received. Offsetting swaps are carried at market value, and any changes in market value are reflected in interest expense or interest income.

If the swap is unmatched, then different treatment will be required. The swap can be marked-to-market and revalued at each reporting date. A cumulative net profit covering all of the profit-making swaps would be recorded as an asset on the balance sheet, and a cumulative net loss covering all of the loss-making swaps would be recorded as a liability on the balance sheet. Alternatively, the aggregate lower-of-cost-or-market (higher-of-proceeds-or-market) approach may be used. In other words, net gains or losses on the swaps are treated as a portfolio, with aggregate net losses being realized immediately and aggregate net gains deferred. On each rollover date, swap payments are normally netted off, but net swap payments are not recorded in income, because they will already have been partly realized.

On the termination of a swap, any profit or loss will be charged to income or expense for the period. If a termination has left another swap position unmatched, then the remaining swap will be dealt with in accordance with the firm's normal accounting policies. If the termination is a result of a default by a counterparty, then the uncollected receivables must be recorded.

During the term of the swap, the swap may be accounted for in the accounting policy note to the financial statements. In November 1987, the Financial Accounting Standards Board released an exposure draft called Exposure Draft, Disclosure of Financial Instruments making proposals on footnote disclosures. They include disclosure of credit risk, disclosure of future cash receipts and payments, disclosure of interest rate information and disclosure of market value information.

The treatment of currency swaps by intermediaries is dealt with under FAS Statement 52 – Foreign Currency Translation. The currency swap is marked-to-market using the forward rates. In the case of multi-currency swaps, gains and losses are accounted for in income or expense. A cumulative net profit covering all of the profit-making swaps would be recorded as an asset on the balance sheet, and a cumulative net loss covering all of the loss-making swaps would be recorded as a liability on the balance sheet.

In the case of a corporate swap user, if a firm issues debt coupled with a swap to change the structure, the original debt issue must still be shown on the balance sheet carried at cost. The swap may be accounted for in the notes to the financial statements so the shareholders are not misled. During the term of the swap, the net settlement can be shown as an adjustment of interest expense. Matched swaps are not marked-to-market regardless of whether they are showing a profit or a loss. The reason for this is that any gain or loss on the swap should be offset by a gain or loss on the asset or liability.

Terminations of interest rate swaps are dealt with using the guidelines of FAS Statement no. 80 which deals with futures contracts. If gains or losses on a futures position are deferred, then they become part of the carrying value of the hedged asset or liability. On termination of the hedge, the cost or carrying value of the hedged asset or liability is not adjusted. Gains or losses deferred before termination should continue to be deferred until the underlying hedged asset or liability has been disposed of.

Accounting for derivative and similar financial instruments and for hedging activities Under current accounting standards, billions of dollars of derivatives transactions are not reported in financial statements, putting investors at risk because they lack important information about prospective investments. By requiring derivatives to be recognized in the financial statements at fair value, the FASB's proposal would remedy that situation by giving investors relevant information in a transparent, understandable, and useful manner.

In August 1997, the Financial Accounting Standards Board (FASB) proposed changes to its original 1996 proposal for accounting for derivatives. The basic requirement of the draft standard is to report derivatives in the financial statements at fair value. It also permits deferral of gains or losses on derivatives used as hedges if the derivative is effective in offsetting changes in the fair value of the hedged item or the cash flows of the hedged transaction. If the Standard is approved, it will take effect in January 1999.

Larger market participants would be required to supplement the basic financial statements with a fair value balance sheet but without a supplemental income statement. Thus gains and losses on derivative transactions would not be displayed. Since 1986 when the FASB began its work on financial instruments, it has implemented a large part of that approach through several standards involving both recognition of and disclosures about financial instruments.

One of the organization's longer-term objectives is to adopt a comprehensive approach to fair value accounting for all financial instruments. The derivatives and hedging proposal is an additional step toward that objective. Existing practices of accounting for derivatives and hedging are a piecemeal approach, and FASB considers it a larger step in its project on fair value accounting. For the present, a piecemeal fair value in financial statements approach may be preferable to the existing recognition approach under which some financial instruments with very significant potential consequences are not recognized at all. It is only one step, but the approach is consistent and compatible with risk management strategies, and the time has come to give investors improved information.

The Board's derivatives project has been controversial. The Federal Reserve, top banking and other corporate executives, as well as non-profit groups have complained that the Board has not adequately considered the proposal's impact on capital markets or the difficulties that companies will have in implementing the proposal.

Transparency in financial reporting is the most important objective of the accounting standards-setting process and that measurement of financial instruments at fair value is the best answer conceptually. The FASB and the Federal Reserve Board disagree about whether information about fair values of derivative instruments should be reported in the financial statements themselves or in the notes to the financial statements at this time. One of the FASB's fundamental principles is that disclosure in the notes to the financial statements is not a substitute for recognition in the financial statements. For derivatives, this is particularly important because if they are not measured at fair value many will not be recognized at all. The volume of transactions in the derivatives market and the large unexpected losses that a few entities have reported have led to a demand for recognition of derivative transactions, so that investors can appropriately assess the effects of derivatives transactions.

Investors and creditors (as well as issuers of financial statements and their auditors) tend to ascribe less importance to information in the notes than to information in the financial statements. The credibility of financial reporting is extremely important to the proper functioning of capital markets. That credibility suffers when important information like the values of the derivative instruments is relegated to the notes to the financial statements.

The Federal Reserve's concerns about the revised proposal are:

- it is a piecemeal fair value approach that may be misleading because different instruments are measured differently;
- it will result in an increase in volatility of comprehensive income and equity without a real increase in risk;
- it may discourage prudent risk management;
- it will require significant systems changes for entities that use derivatives as hedges; and
- it is not likely to be internationally acceptable.

The FASB's response to these concerns is as follows:

> *The derivatives and hedging proposal is only a step toward fair value accounting for all financial instruments. Existing practices of accounting for derivatives and hedging also are a*

piecemeal approach. One of FASB's longer-term objectives is to adopt a more comprehensive approach. FASB is considering that larger step in its project on fair value accounting. For the present, a piecemeal fair value approach seems to be preferable to the existing piecemeal recognition approach under which some financial instruments with very significant potential consequences are ignored altogether. It is only one step, but the approach is consistent and compatible with risk management objectives, and the time has come to give investors improved information.[15]

The Federal Reserve expressed concerns that investors and creditors may be misled by the FASB's revised proposal. FASB is not convinced that reporting estimates of fair value that may be imprecise could be any more misleading than omitting many derivatives from the balance sheet altogether.

Reporting derivative instruments under the revised proposal would not create volatility, says the FASB. Current reporting practices obscure existing volatility. The FASB proposal would only require reporting of volatility that currently is not reported. For example, reporting the market value changes of a hedge of future cash flows in comprehensive income will change equity, but the FASB believes that the gains and losses from these transactions do affect equity and that to ignore these effects is misleading. Under the FASB's proposal, hedges of the fair value of existing assets or liabilities may affect equity and earnings, but only insofar as the hedge strategy is ineffective in offsetting the fair value changes of the hedged item. The measure of ineffectiveness will be based on management's approach consistent with their strategy. Deferral of gains and losses on items that are not effective as hedges would disguise the real effects of the hedge.

Changes made to the proposal since the exposure draft was issued would significantly reduce the volatility of reported amounts. FASB recognizes that bank regulators have different objectives from investors and creditors and that regulatory capital determinations may involve adjustments from amounts required by generally accepted accounting principles (for example, deferred tax assets). If the regulators so choose, adjustments can be made here as well.

FASB does not intend to influence any entity's use of derivatives. It is not easy to discern strategies that are prudent. In fact, prudence may vary from entity to entity and may be discernible only in hindsight. FASB's goal is to make it easier for investors and creditors to make their own evaluation of the prudence of management's strategies. FASB believes that the existing practice of omitting many derivatives from the financial statements actually may make it easier to conceal imprudent risk management strategies and also may result in less effective internal controls over derivative transactions. Certainly, a few companies have done so until the results were so obvious that they could no longer avoid reporting them.

Many entities will have to make significant systems changes. FASB plans to allow about a year from the date the Statement is issued to the effective date to give those entities time to make the changes. The Federal Reserve expressed concerns that entities with unhedged positions would face fewer requirements than those who enter into hedges. FASB believes this is appropriate. Those entities that choose to enter into hedging transactions should account for them.

FASB is actively participating in both the International Accounting Standards Committee (IASC) process and the process of certain other national standards setters, but it cannot predict the actions of those standards-setting bodies. FASB is aware that the IASC has received comments that suggest an approach similar to its revised proposal. FASB believes that if the US can implement a workable, informative hedge accounting standard, there is a reasonable possibility that international practice will follow its lead. No other group has a satisfactory answer and all are aware of the need. Japan, for example, indicated that it is considering adopting fair value for measuring financial instruments.

No other project is likely to change the conclusions reached in this one in the near term. The fair value project is long term. Even if FASB was willing to deprive investors of important information and wait for that project, reporting fair values of all financial instruments still would not provide a means of reporting hedges of anticipated transactions that would be acceptable to constituents who engage in those transactions.

The Federal Reserve Board's suggested alternative consists of the following elements:

- Historical cost-based financial statements with measurement of derivatives held for trading purposes at fair value and measurement of derivatives used as hedges using a 'simple hedging framework' based on the 'matching principle' that reflects current 'best practices';
- Supplemental fair value based balance sheets for larger organizations actively involved in the markets;
- Expanded guidance on fair value in key areas.

FASB considered those recommendations in some detail. Most of what the Federal Reserve has recommended already is required of most entities by FASB Statement No. 119, Disclosure about Derivative Financial Instruments and Fair Value of Financial Instruments, and

FASB Statement No. 107, Disclosures about Fair Value of Financial Instruments. The Federal Reserve's approach would require repealing those Statements for small entities and reformatting the information for larger ones. FASB sees several disadvantages and difficulties with implementing the Federal Reserve's suggestion.

Financial statements currently are not based on a historical cost framework; rather it is a mixed-attribute framework. For example, FASB Statement No. 115, Accounting for Certain Investments in Debt and Equity Securities, requires that most securities be measured at fair value. FASB strongly believes that repealing Statement 115 would be a step backward and would not be serving investors and creditors. Nor is the proposal a historical cost framework. It is also a mixed-attribute framework because at least trading account securities and perhaps other financial instruments would be reported at fair value.

FASB maintains that the Federal Reserve does not fully describe the 'simple hedging framework,' it envisions. Existing hedge accounting practices are based on complex and arbitrary rules, and they result in different accounting depending primarily on the instrument selected for hedging purposes.

FASB believes that a 'simple hedging framework' is not feasible. Accommodating the many hedging strategies in use today requires either a very complex model or an undisciplined 'free choice' that would result in inconsistencies between companies and consequently could easily mislead investors. FASB has attempted to accommodate as many of those strategies as possible without making the proposal more complex than necessary.

FASB also claims that the Federal Reserve's proposals would result in a loss of information about entities other than major market participants. Statements 107 and 119 already require disclosure of fair values of derivatives and other financial instruments (as do SEC rules). FASB believes it is not appropriate to exempt entities from those requirements, except smaller entities that are already exempt because they have no derivative activity.

The Federal Reserve's suggestions for changes discussed balance sheet information only. Without an income statement, investors and creditors would not have information about the effect of changes in fair values of derivatives on earnings and comprehensive income.

The Federal Reserve is focusing on the larger financial institutions. However, the issue affects many companies that are not large financial institutions. Under the Fed's proposal, investors and creditors would not have any information about derivative activities of entities that are not major market participants despite the fact that even a single transaction may be significant to some of those entities.

The Federal Reserve believes that disclosures in notes to financial statements will encourage entity-wide risk management. Yet, FASB maintains that entity-wide risk management is often difficult for reasons unrelated to accounting rules, in particular, decentralization of authority and operations and the difficulty of timely accumulation of information. FASB does not believe that any accounting standard will encourage entity-wide risk management. Nor is it FASB's goal to achieve that or any other change in management policies.

Competition between fair value and historical cost, which is another of the advantages that the Fed ascribes to in its proposal, is occurring today. Statement 107 and Statement 119 require fair value information and, fair value estimation techniques seem to be improving. Financial statement issuers will have at least two more year ends to disclose fair value information in notes to financial statements before they are required to recognize the fair value of derivatives in their financial statements.

FASB agrees that it is necessary to provide additional guidance on estimating fair values in certain circumstances. The issues mentioned by the Federal Reserve are only a partial list; for example, valuation of insurance liabilities also is an important and difficult issue. As a practical matter, a project like that would take several years to complete. It is within the scope of FASB's fair value project, but to use that project as a substitute for the narrower current project on derivatives and hedging would postpone improved transparency until well into the next century and would deprive investors and creditors of useful information in the meantime.

SUMMARY

Credit risk plays an important role in the swap market. Credit risk may be assessed by evaluating the replacement cost of the swap if the counterparty defaults. From the company's point of view, by entering into a swap, credit lines may be tied up which could potentially jeopardize projects in the future. However, in most cases the flexibility the swap provides in liability management is justification for doing the swap. From the banks' point of view, if a company is using the swap as a hedge, then the transaction with the company may be perceived as less risky.

Because of the perceived risk in the swap market, the Bank of International Settlements, along with the various central banks, have assigned risk weightings on swap transactions in compliance with the capital adequacy requirements. All banks are required to set aside an amount of capital to support a swap portfolio. The capital adequacy requirements have had an impact on swaps trading, and, in particular, complicated multi-leg transactions and currency swaps are now unprofitable for many banks.

Legal risk, default risk and sovereign risk have been the highlights of the swap market in the last few years. The Hammersmith and Fulham case, in which a UK local authority dealt swaps, swaptions and gilt options *ultra vires*, was a protracted battle which has had implications for other local authorities using swap products and has meant huge losses for both British and foreign banks. Although the situation did not pose a threat to London's position as a major financial centre, the prudence of the Bank of England as a regulatory authority was called into question.

Despite the risks and regulations, standardized documentation has made swaps trading far less complicated. The most commonly used form of documentation was written by the International Swaps and Derivatives Association (ISDA), and many active swap participants negotiate master agreements based on ISDA documentation. Other standardized documentation, such as BBAIRS and AIRS exist, but they are limited in their scope and are thus used less often. The standard ISDA documentation contains provisions for payments, tax indemnities, representations and covenants, events of default, termination events, assignments, contractual currencies, multibranch parties, notices, jurisdiction and waiver of immunities. However, one criticism of ISDA documentation is that it is too complex.

How an accountant deals with a swap may be determined by the reason the swap was transacted, and whether it is a matched swap, a hedged swap, an unmatched swap or an offsetting swap. Treatment of swaps will also depend on whether the party executing the swap is a financial institution, financial intermediary or a corporate user. Accountants look at the SSAPs in the United Kingdom and the FASs in the US for indications of how to account for a swap or swap product. The FASB in the US has released a Draft Exposure for accounting for derivatives, which it hopes will be approved and implemented in January 1999.

Notes

1. Keith Wishon and Lorin S. Chevalier. 'Interest rate swaps – your rate or mine?', *Journal of Accountancy*, September 1985.
2. Clifford W. Smith et al. 'The market for interest rate swaps', *Financial Management*, vol. 17, winter 1988, p. 43.
3. ibid., p. 34.
4. ibid.

5. See William D. Kerr. 'Proposed capital requirements for swaps and other interest and exchange rate instruments' in *Swap Finance*, Vol. I, edited by Boris Antl, London: Euromoney Publications, 1988, p. 25.

6. ibid., pp. 26, 31.

7. Louise Ireland. 'Getting a fix with swaps', *Corporate Finance*, no. 47, October 1988, p. 42.

8. SSAP 2 – Disclosure of Accounting Policies, February 1987, pp. 4–5.

9. SSAP 18 – Accounting for Contingencies, February 1987, p. 1.

10. SSAP 18 – Accounting for Contingencies, February 1987, p. 3.

11. SSAP 20 – Foreign Currency Translation, February 1987, p. 2.

12. John Tiner and Joe Conneely. 'Taking swaps into account', *The Treasurer*, vol. 12, no. 2, February 1990, p. 32.

13. The following passage is a direct quote from John Tiner and Joe Conneely, op. cit., p. 34.

14. As of 14 March 1989, the definition of 'UK counterparties exempt from withholding' has been amended to include swap dealers recognized either by the Bank of England or by the The Securities Association, once formal Revenue approval has been secured.

15. Excerpt from a letter from Edmund L. Jenkins, FASB, to Alan Greenspan, Federal Reserve Board, 11 August 1997.

Bibliography

Abdullah, Fuad A. and Bean, Virgilua L. (1988). 'At last, a swaps primer', *Financial Executive*, vol. 4, July/August, pp. 53–7.

Accounting Standards Committee, The (1987). SSAP 2 – Disclosure of Accounting Policies, February, London.

Accounting Standards Committee, The (1987). SSAP 18 – Accounting for Contingencies, February, London.

Accounting Standards Committee, The (1987). SSAP 20 – Foreign Currency Translation, February, London.

Antl, Boris (ed.) (1986, 1988). *Swap Finance, Vols I and II*. London: Euromoney Publications Ltd.

Brown, Keith C. and Smith, Donald J. (1988). 'Recent innovations in interest rate risk management and the reintermediation of commerical banking', *Financial Management*, vol. 17, winter, pp. 45–58.

Courtney, Rohan (1990). 'Whither local authority swaps', *The Treasurer*, vol. 12, no. 2, February, pp. 39, 42.

Das, Satyajit (1989). *Swap Financing*. London: IFR Publishing Ltd.

DeCovny, Sherree and Tacchi, Christine (1991). *Hedging Strategies*. Cambridge: Woodhead-Faulkner (Publishers) Ltd.

The Economist (1990). 'Buddy, can you spare some capital?', vol. 317, no. 7679, 3 November, pp. 117–18.

Hamilton, James (1990). 'An introduction to swap products', *The Treasurer*, vol. 12, no. 2, February, pp. 6–9.

The IFR (1991). 'Derivative instruments', issue 877, 11 May, p. 72.

Ireland, Louise (1988). 'Getting a fix with swaps', *Corporate Finance*, vol. 47, October, pp. 39, 42.

Kersey, Craig (1990). 'Swaps and credit exposure', *The Treasurer*, vol. 12, no. 2, February, pp. 22–5.

Luke, John (1988). 'Interest rate swaps', *Public Finance and Accountancy*, 27 May, pp. 11–14.

Ray, Russ (1989). 'Interest rate swaps that benefit both parties', *Risk Management*, vol. 36, April, pp. 64, 66.

Rue, Joseph C., Tosh, David E. and Francis, William B. (1988). 'Accounting for interest rate swaps', *Management Accounting (NAA)*, vol. 70, July, pp. 43–9.

Smith, Donald J. (1988). 'Measuring the gains from arbitraging the swap market', *Financial Executive*, vol. 4 March/April, pp. 46–9.

Smith, Donald J. and Taggart Jr., Robert A. (1989). 'Bond market innovations and financial intermediation', *Business Horizons*, November/December, pp. 24–34.

Smith Jr., Clifford W., Smithson, Charles W. and Macdonald Wakeman, Lee (1986). 'The evolving market for swaps', *Midland Corporate Finance Journal*, winter, pp. 20–32.

Smith Jr., Clifford W., Smithson, Charles W. and Macdonald Wakeman, Lee (1988). 'The market for interest rate swaps', *Financial Management*, vol. 17, winter, pp. 34–44.

Tiner, John and Conneely, Joe (1990). 'Taking swaps into account', *The Treasurer*, vol. 12, no. 2, February, pp. 30–4.

Wishon, Keith and Chevalier, Lorin S. (1985). 'Interest rate swaps – your rate or mine?', *Journal of Accountancy*, September.

APPENDIX I
CHICAGO MERCANTILE EXCHANGE
DEPOSITORY TRUST CO.[1]

As a Member of the CME Depository Trust Co. (CME DTC), the firm will have access to standardized collateral management and to a menu of complimentary administrative services the Depository offers. Beyond collateral management, Members will have access to electronic trade matching and confirmation services through the Society for Worldwide Interbank Telecommunications (SWIFT), valuation and rate administration via SunGard Capital Markets' Devon Derivatives Systems, global reporting and cashflow netting. By offering these services together, the CME DTC can help Members reduce the administrative demands of both collateral and trade administration.

1) Trade matching

One of the most paper- and labour-intensive back office tasks is trade confirmation matching. This process involves faxing or telexing trade confirmation messages and then collating the counterparties' responses with the original messages to ensure that all discrepancies are accounted for and corrected. When done manually, this process is very time consuming and, given the repetitive nature of the job, prone to human error. Members of the CME DTC, however, take advantage of Accord, SWIFT's electronic confirmation and trade matching service.

The SWIFT interface with the Depository allows CME DTC Members and their counterparties to confirm and match executed transactions with the appropriate SWIFT formatted messages. In cases where both counterparties are Depository Members and the trade has been successfully confirmed and matched, SWIFT forwards images of the matched trade to the Depository, where both sides of the trade are registered.

2) Valuation

The CME DTC uses the Devon Derivatives System not only for position keeping and trade administration, but also to value Members' current position exposures upon request. These valuations can be used for credit support calculations and to provide a 'second opinion' to internal, proprietary valuations. And there is no 'black box' for Members to contend with; all of the Devon System's valuation assumptions – including index term structure definitions, the discount function of these term structures, the calculation of forward rates and the discounting results of cash flows – are made available to Members.

Instrument coverage includes single and cross-currency swaps, caps and floors, and FRAs where full trade detail information is available to the Depository. As a rule, the CME DTC supports valuation where there is a market consensus as to a representative term structure for an index and reliable sources of market prices and rates. The Depository supports all Euro-deposit traded indices – (ie, CAD, DEM, GBP, USD, etc.), US domestic indices (Commercial Paper, Fed Funds, Prime, Treasury Bill, etc.) and various other non-US domestic indices (CAD-BA, DKK-CIBOR, NLG-AIBOR, FRF-PIBOR, etc.)

3) Collateral management

The CME DTC performs administrative tasks to bolster the bank's internal credit support programme and provides an infrastructure that should allow the bank to claim the lowest possible capital charge. The Federal Reserve Board has proposed that financial institutions that collateralize their off-balance sheet derivatives transactions may claim a lower risk weighting against the credit exposure associated with these transactions. Likewise, there are strong indications that other Central Banks are in the process of adopting similar guidelines. Thus, from a regulatory perspective', the incentives to collateralize privately negotiated transactions have never been greater. Similarly, from a business perspective, many banks are interested in extending collateralization because of its credit risk management and relationship benefits.

The CME DTC can help the bank take advantage of both these regulatory and business benefits by storing and processing the attributes of its credit support agreements. The CME DTC stores Master Agreement Profiles for all Members. These contain all of a Member's bilateral credit support attributes for a given counterparty. If a Member has multiple agreements with a given counterparty, then these separate agreements are maintained as distinct agreement profiles. The Depository supports the calculation of credit support requirements for positions that fall under established Master Agreement Profiles and where both counterparties are CME DTC Members. Members may also register two different types of 'threshold' limits within the Depository: a sliding amount based on S&P and/or Moody's credit ratings, or an explicit threshold amount. The Depository automatically adjusts collateral threshold limits and minimum transfer amounts, as specified in the Master Agreement Profiles, and requests collateral adjustments accordingly.

Once credit support requirements have been determined, the Depository sends Members a report detailing the demand amount. Members deliver sufficient collateral to meet this demand requirement to the CME DTC through private banking sector sub-custodians. These sub-custodians are selected in part because they do not have competitive proprietary trading activities. The Depository is notified of the delivery of collateral through standard SWIFT messages sent by the Member and confirmed by the sub-custodians. Upon receipt of these messages, deposits are recorded in the CME DTC Asset Management System.

The CME DTC holds collateral as a trustee for Members and counterparties. Members transfer title of their collateral to the Depository, which gives the CME DTC the flexibility to manage it in the most efficient manner. The CME DTC pools the collateral. Each day, the Depository calculates the US dollar equivalent of the pooled collateral and allocates to each Member the appropriate portion based on that Member's deposited assets in the Depository.

Each Member's portion of the pool is referred to as its 'Depositor Monetized Value' (DMV). DMV functions like a generic 'currency' within the CME DTC. Standardizing and homogenizing different collateral assets into DMV enables the Depository to transfer collateral entitlements and enables Members to retransfer collateral among themselves more efficiently. The CME DTC executes collateral transfers simply by crediting and debiting DMV in the appropriate Member accounts.

For example, when a Member transfers collateral to the Depository, the equivalent DMV is credited to the Member's Primary Account. If that Member owes collateral within the CME DTC, their Primary Account is debited, and the secured Member's Credit Support Account is credited.

Recognizing the importance of collateral optimization, the Depository is structured to enable the Members to utilize collateral as efficiently as possible. Members may reuse the DMV transferred to their accounts.

4) Global reporting

The Depository offers a selection of end-of-day activity statements that are transmitted to Members via SWIFT. Reporting options include a global summary report, designed to meet the needs of 'Home Office' executives, that includes aggregate activity for all subsidiary units or a pre-selected subset of units. Members can provide the Depository with standing instructions regarding the level of detail these reports might contain. For example, instructions might specify that summary level information is always transmitted while trade detail reports are submitted only upon request.

5) Netting cash flow payments

The Depository offers and optional Payments Netting Service to net cash flow payments associated with interMember trades down to a single pay or collect per currency, per value date, equal to the amount owed to or owed from all of the other participating Members. We believe this payments netting service complies with the BIS Lamfalussy Standards for netting facilities and with indigenous payment systems for the currencies that the CME DTC nets.

6) Administration of resets and fixings

The Depository uses SunGard Capital Markets' Devon Derivatives System to track applicable floating index resets and calculate the respective fixing for designated trades. As with the Depository's Valuation Service, the CME DTC supports a wide variety of products and floating indices including SWIFT-supported products, single and cross-currency swaps, caps and floors, FRAs, and floating indices that have a market-accepted source and determination in terms. The Depository supports all documented floating-rate options under the latest ISDA definitions.

This service can be used to supplement the valuation and netting services, both of which are dependent on accurate rate-fixing results for floating indices. The Depository transmits all related data and position results back to the subscribing Members in their end-of-day activity statements.

How the CME DTC system works

To physically support its services, the Depository blends the latest software systems from SWIFT, SunGard Capital Markets and the CME. SWIFT primarily supports the interface between Members, the Depository and its subcustodians through the following three products: SWIFT FIN (Message/trade position routing); SWIFT Accord (Trade confirmation matching and third-party notification); and SWIFT IFT (Activity statement distribution).

SunGard Capital Markets' Devon Derivatives System is used for position keeping and valuation. Additionally, the Depository incorporates modules drawn from the CME's Clearing 21 project. These applications support banking transactions, collateral asset valuation, interest accrual on CME DTC Common Trust Funds and collateral allocation for Member requirements. The modules in use at the Depository already support the CME Clearing House, which typically manages over $9 billion in performance bond collateral in multiple currencies on any given day.

The Members' Operating Agreement, which constitutes a binding contract among CME DTC Members and between Members and the CME DTC, specifies standards governing the rights and responsibilities of both Members and the Depository. The Manual of Operations provides detailed instructions for day-to-day processing and for the resolution of various operational contingencies.

Both the Members' Operating Agreement and the Manual of Operations include general guidelines for the practice of collateral management. These guidelines do not disturb existing bilateral Master Agreements, but provisions in the member's Operating Agreement are not used to supplement these bilateral agreements. The content of both the Members' Operating Agreement and the Manual of Operations has been shaped in cooperation with the Depository's Charter Members, who represent the leading Market Professionals in the derivatives industry.

Note

1. At the time of writing, the CME DTC is not operational.

Bibliography

CME Depository Trust Co. (1997). *The Future of Collateral Management*. Chicago: Chicago Mercantile Exchange, pp. 3–6, 8–9.

APPENDIX II
INTERNATIONAL SWAPS AND
DERIVATIVES ASSOCIATION, INC.
(ISDA) AGREEMENTS

INTEREST RATE SWAP
AGREEMENT (1987)

Dated as of ....

.... and

have entered and/or anticipate entering into one or more transactions (each a 'Rate Swap Transaction'). The parties agree that each Rate Swap Transaction will be governed by terms and conditions set forth in this document (which includes the schedule (the 'Schedule')) and in the documents (each a 'Confirmation') exchange between the parties confirming such Rate Swap Transactions. Each Confirmation constitutes a supplement to and forms parts of this document and will be read and construed as one with this document, so that this document and all the Confirmations constitute a single agreement between the parties (collectively referred to as the 'Agreement'). The parties acknowledge that all Rate Swap Transactions are entered into in reliance on the fact that this document and all Confirmations will form a single agreement between the parties, it being understood that the parties would not otherwise enter into any Rate Swap Transactions.

Accordingly, the parties agree as follows:

1. Interpretation, Code of SWAPS

(a) Definitions.   The terms defined in Section 14 and in the Schedule will have the meanings therein specified for the purpose of this Agreement.

(b) Code of *SWAPS.* This Agreement and each Rate Swap Transaction are subject to the Code of Standard Wording, Assumptions and Provisions for Swaps, 1986 Edition (as published by the International Swap Dealers Association, Inc.) (the 'Code'), and will be governed in all relevant respects by the provisions set forth in the Code, without regard to any amendments to the Code subsequent to the date hereof. The provisions of the Code are incorporated by reference in, and shall be deemed to be a part of, this document and each Confirmation, as if set forth in full in this document or in that Confirmation. This Agreement constitutes a Rate Swap Agreement as that term is used in the Code.

(c) Inconsistency. In the event of any inconsistency between the provisions of this document and the Code, this document will prevail. In the event of any inconsistency between the provisions of any Confirmation and this document, such Confirmation will prevail for the purpose of the relevant Rate Swap Transaction.

2. Payments

(a) Obligations and Conditions. Subject to the payment basis specified below and the other terms and conditions set forth or incorporated by reference in this Agreement (including without limitation Article 10 of the Code) or in a Confirmation, with respect to each Rate Swap Transaction, each party will make each payment specified in that Confirmation as being payable by it by transfer of the relevant amount in freely transferable funds to the account of the other party specified for that Rate Swap Transaction. Unless otherwise provided in a Confirmation, the Fixed Amount or Floating Amount applicable to a Payment Date will be the Fixed Amount or Floating Amount calculated with reference to the Calculation Period ending on, but excluding, the Period End Date (or in the case of the Final Calculation Period, the Termination Date) that coincides with, or corresponds to, that Payment Date.

(b) Change of Account. Either party may change its account to another account in the country originally specified, by giving notice to the other party at least five days prior to a Payment Date for which such change applies.

(c) Netting. The obligations of the parties under this Section 2 will be calculated and payable on the basis of Net Payments. The parties may, if so specified in the Schedule or otherwise, apply Net Payments-

Corresponding Payment Dates to their respective obligations under this Section 2 with effect from the date so specified; provided that, in such case, Net Payments-Corresponding Payment Dates will apply separately to each Office through which a party makes and receives payments as set forth in Section 10.

3. Representations

The representations of the parties (other than those relating to tax matters, if any) are specified below and will be deemed to be repeated at the times set forth in Section 15.1 of the Code:

(a) Basic Representations;

(b) Absence of Certain Events, which in the case of an event or condition that has occurred, is continuing

(c) Absence of Litigation; and

(d) Accuracy of Specified Information.

4. Agreements

The agreements of the parties (other than Tax Covenants, if any) are specified below:

(a) Each party agrees to deliver to the other party any documents specified in the Schedule or a Confirmation as soon as practicable or by the date specified in the Schedule or such Confirmation;

(b) Each party agrees to Maintain Authorizations and Comply with Laws, but in the case of Section 16.1 (f)(i) of the Code only to the extent that each party agrees to use all reasonable efforts; and

(c) Each party agrees to pay any stamp, registration, documentation or similar tax ('Stamp Tax') levied or imposed upon it or in respect of its execution or performance of this Agreement by a jurisdiction in which it is incorporated, organized, managed and controlled, or considered to have its seat, or in which a branch or office through which it is acting for the purpose of this Agreement is located ('Stamp Tax Jurisdiction') and will indemnify the other party against any Stamp Tax levied or imposed upon the other party or in respect of the other party's execution or performance of this Agreement by any such Stamp Tax Jurisdiction which is not also a Stamp Tax Jurisdiction with respect to the other party.

5. Events of Default and Termination Events

The Events of Default and Termination Events with respect to each party are specified below. The occurrence of any Event of Default or Termination Event with respect to a Specified Entity of a party will constitute an Event of Default or Termination Event with respect to such party.

(a) Events of Default.

(i)   Failure To Pay following a Cure Period of three Business Days After Notice;

(ii)   Breach of Covenant following a Cure Period of thirty days After Notice;

(iii)   Credit Support Default which in the case of Section 11.7(b)(i) of the Code is continuing after any applicable grace period has elapsed;

(iv)   Misrepresentation;

(v)   Default Under Specified Swaps;

(vi)   If Cross-Default is specified in the Schedule as applying to the party, such term will mean: (I) the occurrence or existence of an event or condition in respect of such party or any applicable Specified Entity under one or more agreements or instruments relating to Specified Indebtedness of such party or any such Specified Entity in an agreement amount of not less than the Threshold Amount (as specified in the Schedule) which has resulted in such Specified Indebtedness becoming, or becoming capable at such time of being declared, due and payable under such agreements or instruments before it would otherwise have been due and payable; or (2) the failure by such party or any such Specified Entity to make one or more payments at maturity in an aggregate amount of not less than the Threshold Amount under such agreements or instruments (after giving effect to any applicable grace period);

(vii)   Bankruptcy, which will mean the occurrence of any of the following events with respect to a party or any applicable Specified Entity: such party or any such Specified Entity (1) is dissolved; (2) becomes insolvent or fails or is unable or admits in writing its inability generally to pay its debts as they become due; (3) makes a general assignment, arrangement or composition with or for the benefit of its creditors; (4) institutes or has instituted against it a proceeding seeking a judgment of insolvency or bankruptcy or any other relief under any bankruptcy or insolvency law or other similar law affecting creditors' rights, or a petition is presented for the winding-up or liquidation of the party or any such Specified Entity, and, in the case of any such proceeding or petition instituted or presented against it, such proceeding or petition (A) results in a judgment of insolvency or bankruptcy or the entry of an order for relief or the making of an order for the winding-up or liquidation of the party or such Specified Entity or (B) is not dismissed, discharged, stayed or restrained in each case within 30 days of the institution or presentation thereof; (5) has a resolution passed for its winding-up or liquidation; (6) seeks or becomes subject to the appointment of an administrator, receiver, trustee, custodian or other similar official for it or for all or substantially all its assets (regardless of how brief such appointment may be, or whether any obligations are promptly assumed by another entity or whether any other event described in this clause (6) has occurred and is continuing); (7) any event occurs with respect to the party or any such Specified Entity which, under the applicable laws of any jurisdiction, has an analogous effect to any of the events specified in clauses (1) to (6) (inclusive); or (8) takes any action in furtherance of, or indicating its consent to, approval of, or acquiescence in, any of the foregoing acts; other than in the case of clause (1) or (5) or, to the extent it relates to those clauses, clause (8), for the purpose of a consolidation, amalgamation or merger which would not constitute a Merger Without Assumption; or

(viii) Merger Without Assumption, which will mean that a party consolidates or amalgamates with, or merges into, or transfers all or substantially all its assets to, another entity and, at the time of such consolidation, amalgamation, merger or transfer:

(1) the resulting, surviving or transferee entity fails to assume all the obligations of such party under this Agreement by operation of law or pursuant to an agreement reasonably satisfactory to the other party to this Agreement; or

(2) the benefits of any Credit Support Document relating to this Agreement fail to extend (without the consent of the other party) to the performance by such resulting, surviving or transferee entity of its obligations under this Agreement.

(b) Termination Events

(i)   Illegality;

(ii)   Tax Event, which will mean either:

(1) the party (which will be the Affected Party) will be required

on the next succeeding Payment Date to pay to the other party an additional amount in respect of an Indemnifiable Tax under Section 19.1(b) of the Code (except in respect of default interest) as a result of a Change in Tax Law; or

(2) there is a substantial likelihood that the party (which will be the Affected Party) will be required on the next succeeding Payment Date to pay to the other party an additional amount in respect of an Indemnifiable Tax under Section 19.1(b) of the Code (except in respect of default interest) and such substantial likelihood results from an action taken by a taxing authority, or brought in a court of competent jurisdiction, on or after the Trade Date of such Rate Swap Transaction (regardless of whether such action was taken or brought with respect to a party to this Agreement);

(iii) Tax Event Upon Merger, which will mean the party (the 'Burdened Party') on the next succeeding Payment Date will either (1) be required to pay to the other party an additional amount in respect of an Indemnifiable Tax under Section 19.l(b) of the Code (except in respect of default interest) or (2) receive a payment from which an amount has been deducted or withheld for or on account of any Indemnifiable Tax in respect of which the other party is not required to pay an additional amount, in either case as a result of a party consolidating or amalgamating with, or merging into, or transferring all or substantially all its assets to, another entity (which will be the Affected Party) where such action does not constitute a Merger Without Assumption; or

(iv) If Credit Event Upon Merger is specified in the Schedule as applying to the party, such term will mean that such party ('X') consolidates or amalgamates with, or merges into, or transfers all or substantially all its assets to, another entity and such action does not constitute a Merger Without Assumption but the creditworthiness of the resulting, surviving or transferee entity (which will be the Affected Party) is materially weaker than that of X immediately prior to such action.

(c) Other provisions with respect to Events of Default and Termination Events are as follows:

(i) Limited Early Termination will apply to all Termination Events other than Credit Event Upon Merger.

(ii) If an event or circumstance which would otherwise constitute or give rise to an Event of Default also constitutes an Illegality, it will be treated as an Illegality and will not constitute an Event of Default.

6. Early Termination

(a) Right to Terminate Following Event of Default. A party entitled to designate an Early Termination Date in respect of an Event of Default may do so by giving notice to the other party of the Early Termination Date not more than 20 days prior to the date so designated (which date may not be earlier than the date such notice is effective); provided, however, that Immediate Early Termination will apply with respect to an Event of Default under Section 5(a) (vii) and, in the case of an Event of Default under clause (4) thereof, the Early Termination Date shall be deemed to have occurred as of the time immediately preceding the institution of the relevant proceeding or the presentation of the relevant petition.

(b) Right to Terminate Following Termination Event

(i)   Notice. Upon the occurrence of a Termination Event, an Affected Party will, promptly upon becoming aware of the same, notify the other party thereof, specifying the nature of such Termination Event and the Affected Transactions relating thereto. The Affected Party will also give such other information to the other party with regard to such Termination Event as the other party may reasonably require.

(ii)   Transfer to Avoid Termination Event. Notwithstanding Section 18.3 of the Code, if either an Illegality under Section 11.8(a) (i) of the Code or a Tax Event occurs and there is only one Affected Party, or if a Tax Event Upon Merger occurs and the Affected Party is the Burdened Party, the Affected Party will as a condition to its right to designate an Early Termination Date use all reasonable efforts (which will not require such party to incur a loss, excluding immaterial, incidental expenses) to transfer within 20 days after the Affected Party gives notice under Section 6(b) (i) all its rights and obligations under this Agreement in respect of the Affected Transactions to another of its offices, branches or Affiliates so that such Termination Event ceases to exist.

If the Affected Party is not able to make such a transfer it will give notice to the other party to that effect within such 20-day period, whereupon the other party may effect such a transfer within 30 days after the notice is given under Section 6(b) (i).

Any such transfer by a party under this Section 6(b) (ii) will be subject to and conditional upon the prior written consent of the other party, which consent will not be withheld if such other party's policies in effect at such time would permit it to enter into swap transactions with the transferee on the terms proposed.

(iii)   Two Affected Parties. If an Illegality under Section 11.8(a) (i) of the Code or a Tax Event occurs and there are two Affected Parties, each party will use all reasonable efforts to reach agreement within 30 days after notice thereof is given under Section 6(b) (i) on action that would cause such Termination Event to cease to exist.

(iv)   Right to Terminate. Notwithstanding Section 11.6 of the Code, if:

(1)   a transfer under Section 6(b) (ii) or an agreement under Section 6(b) (iii), as the case may be, has not been effected with respect to all Affected Transactions within 30 days after an Affected Party gives notice under Section 6(b) (i); or

(2)   an Illegality under Section 11.8(a) (ii) of the Code or a Credit Event Upon Merger occurs, or a Tax Event Upon Merger occurs and the Burdened Party is not the Affected Party, either party in the case of an Illegality, the Burdened Party in the case of a Tax Event Upon Merger, any Affected Party in the case of a Tax Event, or the party which is not the Affected Party in the case of a Credit Event Upon Merger, will be the party entitled to designate an Early Termination Date. Such party may designate an Early Termination Date in respect of all Affected Transactions by giving notice not more than 20 days prior to the date so designated (which date may not be earlier than the date such notice is effective).

(c) Effect of Designation. Upon the effectiveness of notice designating an Early Termination Date (or the deemed occurrence of an Early Termination Date), the obligations of the parties to make any further payments under Section 2 in respect of the Terminated Transactions will terminate, but without prejudice to the other provisions of this Agreement.

(d) Calculations. The amount calculated as being payable under Section 6(e) will be due on the day that notice of the amount payable is effective (in the case of an Early Termination Date which is designated or deemed to occur as a result of an Event of Default) and not later than the day which is two Business Days after the day on which notice of the amount payable is effective (in the case of an Early Termination Date which is designated as a result of a Termination Event). Such notice shall specify the account for payment.

Such amount will be paid together with (to the extent permitted under applicable law) interest thereon from (and including) the relevant Early Termination Date to (but excluding) the relevant due date, calculated as follows:

(i) if notice is given designating an Early Termination Date or if an Early Termination Date is deemed to occur, in either case as a result of an Event of Default, at the Default Rate; or

(ii) if notice is given designating an Early Termination Date as a result of a Termination Event, at the Default Rate minus the Default Spread.

Such interest will be computed on the basis of Compounding using daily Compounding Dates, as if the rate specified were a Floating Rate, such period were a Calculation Period and the amount due were a Notional Amount.

(e) Payments on Early Termination.

(i) Amount Payable. The amount payable in respect of an Early Termination Date will be calculated as follows:

(1) If there is a Defaulting Party, the Defaulting Party will pay to the other party the excess, if a positive number, of (A) the sum of (i) the amount determined in accordance with Agreement Value-Limited Two Way Payments, calculated on the basis of Aggregation (or, if the Aggregate Market Quotation calculated in determining such amount is less than zero, the amount by which such Aggregate Market Quotation is less than zero, expressed as a negative number) and (ii) the Unpaid Amounts due to the other party over (B) the Unpaid Amounts due to the Defaulting Party; and

(2) if an Early Termination Date occurs as a result of a Termination Event, the payment to be made will be the amount equal to (A) the sum of (i) the amount determined in accordance with Agreement Value-Limited Two Way Payments, calculated on the basis of Aggregation and (ii) the Unpaid Amounts due to the party ('X') entitled to receive a payment under clause (i) minus (B) the Unpaid Amounts due to the other party ('Y'). If the resulting amount is a

positive number, Y will pay such amount to X. If the resulting amount is negative, X will pay the absolute value of such amount to Y; and

(3) for purposes of the foregoing clauses (1) and (2), if Market Quotation is not, or cannot be, determined with respect to a Rate Swap Transaction, the alternative measure of damages with respect to such Rate Swap Transaction will be Indemnification-Limited Two Way Payments; provided that, (A) in the case of clause (1) (A) (i) above, the amount, if any, by which Loss is less than zero will be given effect and (B) in the case of a Termination Event where there is only one Affected Party, Indemnification-Limited Two Way Payments will be computed without regard to the Loss of the Affected Party.

(ii) Adjustment for Bankruptcy. In circumstances where an Early Termination Date is deemed to occur as a result of Immediate Early Termination, the amount determined under Section 6(e) (i) will be subject to such adjustments as are appropriate and permitted by law to reflect any payments made by one party to the other under this Agreement (and retained by such other party) during the period from the relevant Early Termination Date to the date for payment determined under Section 6(d).

(iii) Pre-Estimate of Loss. The parties agree that the amounts recoverable under this Section 6(e) are a reasonable pre-estimate of loss and not a penalty. Such amounts are payable for the loss of bargain and the loss of protection against future risks and except as otherwise provided in this Agreement neither party will be entitled to recover any additional damages as a consequence of such losses.

7. Transfer

Subject to Section 6(b) and to any exception provided in the Schedule, neither this Agreement nor any interest or obligation in or under this Agreement may be transferred by either party without the prior written consent of the other party (other than pursuant to a consolidation or amalgamation with, or merger into, or transfer of all or substantially all its assets to, another entity) and any purported transfer without such consent will be void.

8. Contractual Currency

All payments under this Agreement will be made in Dollars. In connection with a demand for payment of any additional amount under Section 18.1 of the Code, it will be sufficient for a party to demonstrate that it would have suffered a loss had an actual exchange or purchase been made.

9. Miscellaneous

(a) Entire Agreement. This Agreement constitutes the entire agreement and understanding of the parties with respect to its subject matter and supersedes all oral communications and prior writings with respect thereto.

(b) Amendments. No amendment, modification or waiver in respect of this Agreement will be effective unless in writing and executed by each of the parties or confirmed by an exchange of telexes.

(c) Survival of Obligations. Except as provided in Section 6(c), the obligations of the parties under this Agreement will survive the termination of any Rate Swap Transaction.

(d) Remedies Cumulative. Except as provided in this Agreement, the rights, powers, remedies and privileges provided in this Agreement are cumulative and not exclusive of any rights, powers, remedies and privileges provided by law.

(e) Confirmations. A confirmation may be executed in counterparts or created by an exchange of telexes, which in either case will be sufficient for all purposes to evidence a binding supplement to this Agreement. Any such counterpart or telex will specify that it constitutes a Confirmation.

10. Multibranch Parties

If a party is specified as a Multibranch Party in the Schedule, such Multibranch Party may make and receive payments under any Rate Swap Transaction through any of its branches or offices listed in the Schedule (each an 'Office'). The Office through which it so makes and receives payments for the purpose of any Rate Swap Transaction will be specified in the relevant Confirmation and any change of Office for such purpose requires the prior written consent of the other party. Each Multibranch Party represents to the other party that, notwithstanding the place of payment, the obligations of each Office are for all purposes under this Agreement the obligations of such Multibranch Party. This representation will be deemed to be repeated by such Multibranch Party on each Trade Date.

11. Credit Support Document

If a Credit Support Document is specified with respect to a party in the Schedule, the obligations of such party under this Agreement and in respect of each Rate Swap Transaction will be secured or guaranteed in accordance with the provisions of that Credit Support Document.

12. Tax Matters

(a) Representations and Covenants. The parties make the following Tax Covenant: Give Notice of Breach of Payee Tax Representation or Tax Covenant. In addition, the parties make the Payee Tax Representations, with Withholding Tax Representation and the Tax Covenants specified in the Schedule. In addition, at all times during the Term of any Rate Swap Transaction, each party makes to the other party, and to any Specified Entity of the other party, the representations specified in the Schedule as 'Payor Tax Representations'. Unless otherwise specified (i) all Payee Tax Representations, Payor Tax Representations, the Withholding Tax Representation and all Tax Covenants made by a party will apply to each Office of the party and (ii) all Payee Tax Representations will be subject to the occurrence of a Change in Tax Law.

(b) Exempt From Withholding. If used for purposes of specifying the Withholding Tax Representation of a party in the Schedule, 'Exempt from Withholding' will have the meaning set forth in the Code; provided that, such representation will apply to the jurisdiction from or through which a payment is made, as well as the jurisdictions specified in Section 19.3 of the Code.

(c) Recognized Bank. If used for purposes of specifying Payee Tax Representations or Payor Tax Representations of a party in the Schedule, 'Recognized Bank' means the party represents that it is a bank recognized by the United Kingdom Inland Revenue as carrying on a bona fide banking business in the United Kingdom, is entering into this Agreement in the ordinary course of such business and will bring into account payments made and received under this Agreement in computing its income for United Kingdom tax purposes.

(d) Provide U.S. Tax Forms if Required. If used for purposes of specifying Tax Covenants of a party in the Schedule, 'Provide U.S. Tax Forms if Required' means that the party agrees to complete, accurately and in a manner reasonably satisfactory to the other party, and to execute and deliver to the other party, a United States Internal Revenue Service Form 4224, or any successor form, in respect of any payments received or to be received by that party in connection with the Agreement that are effectively connected or otherwise attributable to its conduct of a trade or business in the United States (i) before the first payment date on which any such payment is or may be so connected or attributable, (ii) promptly upon reasonable demand by the other party, and (iii) promptly upon learning that any such form previously provided has become obsolete or incorrect.

13. Service of Process

Each party irrevocably appoints the party specified in the Schedule, if any, as its agent for service of process. If for any reason a party's agent for service of process is unable to act as such, such party will promptly notify the other party and within 30 days appoint a substitute agent for service of process acceptable to the other party. The parties irrevocably consent to service of process given in accordance with the notice provisions of Article 14 of the Code and this Agreement. Nothing in this Section will affect the right of either party to serve process in any other manner permitted by law.

14. Definitions

As used in this Agreement:

'Affected Transactions' means (a) with respect to any Termination Event to which Limited Early Termination applies under Section 5(c) (i) of this Agreement, all Rate Swap Transactions affected by the occurrence of such Termination Event and (b) with respect to any other Termination Event, all Rate Swap Transactions.

'Default Rate' means a rate per annum determined in accordance with the Federal Funds Floating Rate Option plus the Default Spread, using daily Reset Dates. For purposes of Section 10.3 of the Code, the Default Rate will be applied on the basis of Compounding as if the overdue amount were a Notional Amount and using daily Compounding Dates, and interest will accrue and be payable before as well as after judgment.

'Default Spread' will have the meaning specified in the Schedule.

'Illegality' will have the meaning set forth in Section 11.8 of the Code; provided that, if an event that would otherwise constitute an illegality results from a breach by the party of its obligations under Section 16.1(f) (i) of the Code, such event will not be deemed to be an illegality.

'Indemnifiable Tax' will have the meaning set forth in the Code; provided that, (a) references to the recipient of a payment shall be considered also to refer to a person related to the recipient and (b) the last clause of the definition of 'Indemnifiable Tax' in Section 19.5(d) of the Code shall be considered to refer to a Credit Support Document as well as a Rate Swap Agreement.

'law' means, with respect to tax matters, any treaty, law, rule or regulation, as modified by the practice of any relevant governmental revenue authority.

'Specified Entity' will have the meaning set forth in the Schedule.

'Specified Indebtedness' means any obligation (whether present or future, contingent or otherwise, as principal or surety or otherwise) in respect of borrowed money.

'Specifed Swap' means any rate swap or currency exchange trans-action now existing or hereafter entered into between one party to this Agreement (or any applicable Specified Entity) and the other party to this Agreement (or any applicable Specified Entity).

'Terminated Transactions' means (a) with respect to any Early Termin-ation Date occurring as a result of a Termination Event, all Affected Transactions and (b) with respect to any Event Termination Date occurring as a result of an Event of Default, all Rate Swap Transactions, which in either case are in effect as of the time immediately preceding the effectiveness of the notice designating such Early Termination Date (or, in the case of Immediate Early Termination, in effect as of the time immediately preceding such Early Termination Date).

'Unpaid Amounts' owing to any party means, with respect to any Early Termination Date, the aggregate of the amounts that became due and payable (or that would have become due and payable but for Section 10.2 of the Code or the designation or occurrence of such Early Termination Date) to such party under Section 2 in respect of all Terminated Transactions by reference to all Calculation Periods ended on or prior to such Early Termination Date and which remain unpaid as at such Early Termination Date, together with (to the extent permitted under applicable law and in lieu of any interest calculated under Section 10.3 of the Code) interest thereon from (and including) the date such amount became due and payable or would have become due and payable to (but excluding) such Early Termination Date, calculated as follows:

(a) in the case of amounts that became so due and payable by a Defaulting Party, at the Default Rate; and

(b) in the case of all other such amounts, at the Default Rate minus the Default Spread.

Such interest will be computed on the basis of Compounding using daily Compounding Dates, as if the rate specified were a Floating Rate, such period were a Calculation Period and the amount due were a Notional Amount.

IN WITNESS WHEREOF the parties have executed this document as of the date specified on the first page of this document.

....

(Name of party)   (Name of party)

By: ....   By: ....

Name: Name:

Title: Title:

INTEREST RATE AND CURRENCY EXCHANGE AGREEMENT (1987)

Dated as of ....

.... and ....

have entered and/or anticipate entering into one or more transactions (each a 'Swap Transaction'). The parties agree that each Swap Transaction will be governed by terms and conditions set forth in this document (which includes the schedule (the 'Schedule')) and in the documents (each a 'Confirmation') exchanged between the parties confirming such Swap Transactions. Each Confirmation constitutes a supplement to and forms part of this document and will be read and construed as one with this document, so that this document and all the Confirmations constitute a single agreement between the parties (collectively referred to as the 'Agreement'). The parties acknowledge that all Swap Transactions are entered into in reliance on the fact that this document and all Confirmations will form a single agreement between the parties, it being understood that the parties would not otherwise enter into any Swap Transactions.

Accordingly, the parties agree as follows:

1. Interpretation

(a) Definitions. The terms defined in Section 14 and in the Schedule will have the meanings therein specified for the purpose of this Agreement.

(b) Inconsistency. In the event of any inconsistency between the provisions of any Confirmation and this document, such Confirmation will prevail for the purpose of the relevant Swap Transaction.

2. Payments

(a) Obligations and Conditions.

(i)   Each party will make each payment specified in each Confirmation as being payable by it.

(ii)   Payments under this Agreement will be made not later than the due date for value on that date in the place of the account specified in the relevant Confirmation or otherwise pursuant to this Agreement, in freely transferable funds and in the manner customary for payments in the required currency.

(iii) Each obligation of each party to pay any amount due under Section 2(a) (i) is subject to (1) the condition precedent that no Event of Default or Potential Event of Default with respect to the other party has occurred and is continuing and (2) each other applicable condition precedent specified in this Agreement.

(b) Change of Account. Either party may change its account by giving notice to the other party at least five days prior to the due date for payment for which such change applies.

(c) Netting. If on any date amounts would otherwise be payable:

(i)   in the same currency; and

(ii)   in respect of the same Swap Transaction,

by each party to the other, then, on such date, each party's obligation to make payment of any such amount will be automatically satisfied and discharged and, if the aggregate amount that would otherwise have been payable by one party exceeds the aggregate amount that would otherwise have been payable by the other party, replaced by an obligation upon the party by whom the larger aggregate amount would have been payable to pay to the other party the excess of the larger aggregate amount over the smaller aggregate amount.

If the parties specify 'Net Payments-Corresponding Payment Dates' in a Confirmation or otherwise in this Agreement, sub-paragraph (ii) above will cease to apply to all Swap Transactions with effect from the date so specified (so that a net amount will be determined in respect of all amounts due on the same date in the same currency, regardless of whether such amounts are payable in respect of the same Swap Transaction); provided that, in such case, this Section 2(c) will apply separately to each Office through which a party makes and receives payments as set forth in Section 10.

(d) Deduction or Withholding for Tax.

(i)   Gross-Up. All payments under this Agreement will be made without any deduction or withholding for or on account of any Tax unless such deduction or withholding is required by any applicable law, as modified by the practice of any relevant governmental revenue authority, then in effect. If a party is so required to deduct or withhold, then that party ('X') will:

(1) promptly notify the other party ('Y') of such requirement;

(2) pay to the relevant authorities the full amount required to be deducted or withheld (including the full amount required to be deducted or withheld from any additional amount paid by X to Y under this Section 2(d)) promptly upon the earlier of determining that such deduction or withholding is required or receiving notice that such amount has been assessed against Y;

(3) promptly forward to Y an official receipt (or a certified copy), or other documentation reasonably acceptable to Y, evidencing such payment to such authorities; and

(4) if such Tax is an Indemnifiable Tax, pay to Y, in addition to the payment to which Y is otherwise entitled under this Agreement, such additional amount as is necessary to ensure that the net amount actually received by Y (free and clear of Indemnifiable Taxes, whether assessed against X or Y) will equal the full amount Y would have received had no such deduction or withholding been required. However, X will not be required to pay any additional amount to Y to the extent that it would not be required to be paid but for:

(A) the failure by Y to comply with or perform any agreement contained in Section 4(a) (i) or 4(d); or

(B) the failure of a representation made by Y pursuant to Section 3(f) to be accurate and true unless such failure would not have occurred but for a Change in Tax Law.

(ii) Liability. If:

(1) X is required by any applicable law, as modified by the practice of any relevant governmental revenue authority, to make any deduction or withholding in respect of which X would not be required to pay an additional amount to Y under Section 2(d) (i) (4);

(2) X does not so deduct or withhold; and

(3) a liability resulting from such Tax is assessed directly against X, then, except to the extent Y has satisfied or then satisfies the liability resulting from such Tax, Y will promptly pay to X the amount of such liability (including any related liability for interest, but including any related liability for penalties only if Y has failed to comply with or perform any agreement contained in Section 4(a) (i) or (d)).

(e) Default Interest. A party that defaults in the payment of any amount due will, to the extent permitted by law, be required to pay interest (before as well as after judgment) on such amount to the other party on demand in the same currency as the overdue amount, for the period from (and including) the original due date for payment to (but excluding) the date of actual payment, at the Default Rate. Such interest will be calculated on the basis of daily compounding and the actual number of days elapsed.

3. Representations

Each party represents to the other party (which representations will be deemed to be repeated by each party on each date on which a Swap Transaction is entered into and, in the case of the representations in Section 3(f), at all times until the termination of this Agreement) that:

(a) Basic Representations.

(i)　Status. It is duly organised and validly existing under the laws of the jurisdiction of its organisation or incorporation and, if relevant under such laws, in good standing;

(ii)　Powers. It has the power to execute and deliver this Agreement and any other documentation relating to this Agreement that it is required by this Agreement to deliver and to perform its obligations under this Agreement and any obligations it has under any Credit Support Document to which it is a party and has taken all necessary action to authorize such execution, delivery and performance;

(iii)　No Violation or Conflict. Such execution, delivery and performance do not violate or conflict with any law applicable to it, any provision of its constitutional documents, any order or judgment of any court or other agency of government applicable to it or any of its assets or any contractual restriction binding on or affecting it or any of its assets;

(iv)　Consents. All governmental and other consents that are required to have been obtained by it with respect to this Agreement or any Credit Support Document to which it is a party have been obtained and are in full force and effect and all conditions of any such consents have been complied with; and

(v)　Obligations Binding. Its obligations under this Agreement and any Credit Support Document to which it is a party constitute its legal, valid and binding obligations, enforceable in accordance with their respective terms (subject to applicable bankruptcy, reorganization, insolvency, moratorium or similar laws affecting creditors' rights generally and subject, as to enforceability, to equitable principles of general application [regardless of whether enforcement is sought in a proceeding in equity or at law]).

(b) Absence of Certain Events. No Event of Default or Potential Event of Default or, to its knowledge, Termination Event with respect to it has occurred and is continuing and no such event or circumstance would occur as a result of its entering into or performing its obligations under this Agreement or any Credit Support Document to which it is a party.

(c) Absence of Litigation. There is not pending or, to its knowledge, threatened against it or any of its Affiliates any action, suit or proceeding at law or in equity or before any court, tribunal, governmental body, agency or official or any arbitrator that purports to draw into question, or is likely to affect, the legality, validity or enforceability against it of this Agreement or any Credit Support Document to which it is a party or its ability to perform its obligations under this Agreement or such Credit Support Document.

(d) Accuracy of Specified Information. All applicable information that is furnished in writing by or on behalf of it to the other party and is identified for the purpose of this Section 3(d) in paragraph 2 of Part 3 of the Schedule is, as of the date of the information, true, accurate and complete in every material respect.

(e) Payer Tax Representation. Each representation specified in Part 2 of the Schedule as being made by it for the purpose of this Section 3(e) is accurate and true.

(f) Payee Tax Representations. Each representation specified in Part 2 of the Schedule as being made by it for the purpose of this Section 3(f) is accurate and true.

4. Agreements

Each party agrees with the other that, so long as it has or may have any obligation under this Agreement or under any Credit Support Document to which it is a party:

(a) Furnish Specified Information. It will deliver to the other party:

(i) any forms, documents or certificates relating to taxation specified in Part 3 of the Schedule or any Confirmation; and

(ii) any other documents specified in Part 3 of the Schedule or any Confirmation, by the date specified in Part 3 of the Schedule or such Confirmation or, if none is specified, as soon as practicable.

(b) Maintain Authorizations. It will use all reasonable efforts to maintain in full force and effect all consents of any governmental or other authority that are required to be obtained by it with respect to this Agreement or any Credit Support Document to which it is a party and will use all reasonable efforts to obtain any that may become necessary in the future.

(c) Comply with Laws. It will comply in all material respects with all applicable laws and orders to which it may be subject if failure so to comply would materially impair its ability to perform its obligations under this Agreement or any Credit Support Document to which it is a party.

(d) Tax Agreement. It will give notice of any failure of a representation made by it under Section 3(f) to be accurate and true promptly upon learning of such failure.

(e) Payment of Stamp Tax. It will pay any Stamp Tax levied or imposed upon it or in respect of its execution or performance of this Agreement by a jurisdiction in which it is incorporated, organized, managed and controlled, or considered to have its seat, or in which a branch or office through which it is acting for the purpose of this Agreement is located ('Stamp Tax Jurisdiction') and will indemnify the other party against any Stamp Tax levied or imposed upon the other party or in respect of the other party's execution or performance of this Agreement by any such Stamp Tax Jurisdiction which is not also a Stamp Tax Jurisdiction with respect to the other party.

5. Events of Default and Termination Events

(a) Events of Default. The occurrence at any time with respect to a party or, if applicable, any Specified Entity of such party, of any of the following events constitutes an event of default (an 'Event of Default') with respect to such party:

(i)   Failure to Pay. Failure by the party to pay, when due, any amount required to be paid by it under this Agreement if such failure is not remedied on or before the third Business Day after notice of such failure to pay is given to the party;

(ii) Breach of Agreement. Failure by the party to comply with or perform any agreement or obligation (other than an obligation to pay any amount required to be paid by it under this Agreement or to give notice of a Termination Event or any agreement or obligation under Section 4(a) (i) or 4(d)) to be complied with or performed by the party in accordance with this Agreement if such failure is not remedied on or before the thirtieth day after notice of such failure is given to the party;

(iii) Credit Support Default.

(1) Failure by the party or any applicable Specified Entity to comply with or perform any agreement or obligation to be complied with or performed by the party or such Specified Entity in accordance with any Credit Support Document if such failure is continuing after any applicable grace period has elapsed;

(2) the expiration or termination of such Credit Support Document, or the ceasing of such Credit Support Document to be in full force and effect, prior to the final Scheduled Payment Date of each Swap Transaction to which such Credit Support Document relates without the written consent of the other party; or

(3) the party or such Specified Entity repudiates, or challenges the validity of, such Credit Support Document;

(iv) Misrepresentation. A representation (other than a representation under Section 3(e) or (f)) made or repeated or deemed to have been made or repeated by the other party or any applicable Specified Entity in this Agreement or any Credit Support Document relating to this Agreement proves to have been incorrect or misleading in any material respect when made or repeated or deemed to have been made or repeated;

(v) Default under Specified Swaps. The occurrence of an event of default in respect of the party or any applicable Specified Entity under a Specified Swap which, following the giving of any applicable notice or the lapse of any applicable grace period, has resulted in the designation or occurrence of an early termination date in respect of such Specified Swap;

(vi) Cross Default. If 'Cross Default' is specified in Part 1 of the Schedule as applying to the party, (1) the occurrence or existence of an event or condition in respect of such party or any applicable Specified Entity under one or more agreements or instruments relating to Specified Indebtedness of such party or any such Specified Entity in an aggregate amount of not less than the Threshold Amount (as specified in Part 1 of the Schedule) which has resulted in such Specified Indebtedness becoming, or becoming capable at such time of being declared, due and payable under such agreements or instruments, before it would otherwise have been due and payable or (2) the failure by such party or any such Specified Entity to make one or more payments at maturity in an aggregate amount of not less than the Threshold Amount under such agreements or instruments (after giving effect to any applicable grace period);

(vii) Bankruptcy. The party or any applicable Specified Entity: (1) is dissolved; (2) becomes insolvent or fails or is unable or admits in writing its inability generally to pay its debts as they become due; (3) makes a general assignment, arrangement or composition with or for the benefit of its creditors; (4) institutes or has instituted against it a proceeding seeking a judgment of insolvency or bankruptcy or any other relief under any bankruptcy or insolvency law or other similar law affecting creditors' rights, or a petition is presented for the winding-up or liquidation of the party or any such Specified Entity, and, in case of any such proceeding or petition instituted or presented against it, such proceeding or petition (A) results in a judgment of insolvency or bankruptcy or the entry of an order for relief or the making of an order for the winding-up or liquidation of the party or such Specified Entity or (B) is not dismissed, discharged, stayed or restrained in each case within 30 days of the institution or presentation thereof; (5) has a resolution passed for its winding-up or liquidation; (6) seeks or becomes subject to the appointment of an administrator, receiver, trustee, custodian or other similar official for it or for all or substantially all its assets (regardless of how brief such appointment may be, or whether any obligations are promptly assumed by another entity or whether any event described in this clause (6) has occurred and is continuing); (7) any event occurs with respect to the party or any such Specified Entity which, under the applicable laws of any jurisdiction, has an analogous effect to any of the events specified in clauses (1) to (6) (inclusive); or (8) takes any action in furtherance of, or indicating its consent to, approval of, or acquiescence in, any of the foregoing acts;

other than in the case of clause (1) to (5) or, to the extent it relates to those clauses, clause (8), for the purpose of a consolidation, amalgamation or merger which would not constitute an event described in (viii) below; or

(viii) Merger Without Assumption. The party consolidates or amalgamates with, or merges into, or transfers all or substantially all its assets to, another entity and, at the time of such consolidation, amalgamation, merger or transfer:

(1) the resulting, surviving or transferee entity fails to assume all the obligations of such party under this Agreement by operation of law or pursuant to an agreement reasonably satisfactory to the other party to this Agreement; or

(2) the benefits of any Credit Support Document relating to this Agreement fail to extend (without the consent of the other party) to the performance by such resulting, surviving or transferee entity of its obligations under this Agreement.

(b) Termination Events. The occurrence at any time with respect to a party or, if applicable, any Specified Entity of such party of any event specified below constitutes an Illegality if the event is specified in (i) below, a Tax Event if the event is specified in (ii) below, a Tax Event Upon Merger if the event is specified in (iii) below or a Credit Event Upon Merger if the event is specified in (iv) below:

(i)   Illegality. Due to the adoption of, or any change in, any applicable law or the date on which such Swap Transaction is entered into, or due to the promulgation of, or any change in, the interpretation by any court, tribunal or regulatory authority with competent jurisdiction of any applicable law after such date, it becomes unlawful (other than as a result of a breach by the party of Section 4(b)) for such party (which will be the Affected Party):

(1) to perform any absolute or contingent obligation to make a payment or to receive a payment in respect of such Swap Transaction or to comply with any other material provision of this Agreement relating to such Swap Transaction; or

(2) to perform, or for any applicable Specified Entity to perform, any contingent or other obligation which the party (or such Specified Entity) has under any Credit Support Document relating to such Swap Transaction;

(ii) Tax Event.

(1) The party (which will be the Affected Party) will be required on the next succeeding Scheduled Payment Date to pay to the other party an additional amount in respect of an Indemnifiable Tax under Section 2(d) (i) (4) (except in respect of interest under Section 2(e)) as a result of a Change in Tax Law; or

(2) there is a substantial likelihood that the party (which will be the Affected Party) will be required on the next succeeding

Scheduled Payment Date to pay to the other party an additional amount in respect of an Indemnifiable Tax under Section 2(d) (i) (4) (except in respect of interest under Section 2(e)) and such substantial likelihood results from an action taken by a taxing authority, or brought in a court of competent jurisdiction, on or after the date on which such Swap Transaction was entered into (regardless of whether such action was taken or brought with respect to a party to this Agreement);

(iii) Tax Event Upon Merger. The party (the 'Burdened Party') on the next succeeding Scheduled Payment Date will either (1) be required to pay an additional amount in respect of an Indemnifiable Tax under Section 2(d) (i) (4) (except in respect of interest under Section 2(e)) or (2) receive a payment from which an amount has been deducted or withheld for or on account of any Indemnifiable Tax in respect of which the other party is not required to pay an additional amount, in either case as a result of a party consolidating or amalgamating with, or merging into, or transferring all or substantially all its assets to, another entity (which will be the Affected Party) where such action does not constitute an event described in Section 5(a) (viii); or

(iv) Credit Event Upon Merger. If 'Credit Event Upon Merger' is specified in Part 1 of the Schedule as applying to the party, such party ('X') consolidates or amalgamates with, or merges into, or transfers all or substantially all its assets to, another entity and such action does not constitute an event described in Section 5(a) (viii) but the creditworthiness of the resulting, surviving or transferee entity (which will be the Affected Party) is materially weaker than that of X immediately prior to such action.

(c) Event of Default and Illegality . If an event or circumstance which would otherwise constitute or give rise to an Event of Default also constitutes an Illegality, it will be treated as an Illegality and will not constitute an Event of Default.

6. Early Termination

(a) Right to Terminate Following Event of Default. If at any time an Event of Default with respect to a party (the 'Defaulting Party') has occurred and is then continuing, the other party may, by not more than 20 days notice to the Defaulting Party specifying the relevant Event of Default, designate a day not earlier than the day such notice is effective as an Early Termination Date in respect of all outstanding

Swap Transactions. However, an Early Termination Date will be deemed to have occurred in respect of all Swap Transactions immediately upon the occurrence of any Event of Default specified in Section 5(a) (vii) (1), (2), (3), (5), (6), (7) or (8) and as of the time immediately preceding the institution of the relevant proceeding or the presentation of the relevant petition upon the occurrence of any Event or Default specified in Section 5(a) (vii) (4).

(b) Right to Terminate Following Termination Event.

(i)   Notice. Upon the occurrence of a Termination Event, an Affected Party will, promptly upon becoming aware of the same, notify the other party thereof, specifying the nature of such Termination Event and the Affected Transactions relating thereto. The Affected Party will also give such other information to the other party with regard to such Termination Event as the other party may reasonably require.

(ii) Transfer to Avoid Termination Event. If either an Illegality under Section 5(b) (i) (1) or a Tax Event occurs and there is only one Affected Party, or if a Tax Event Upon Merger occurs and the Burdened Party is the Affected Party, the Affected Party will as a condition to its right to designate an Early Termination Date under Section 6(b) (iv) use all reasonable efforts (which will not require such party to incur a loss, excluding immaterial, incidental expenses) to transfer within 20 days after it gives notice under Section 6(b) (i) all its rights and obligations under this Agreement in respect of the Affected Transactions to another of its offices, branches or Affiliates so that such Termination Event ceases to exist.

If the Affected Party is not able to make such a transfer it will give notice to the other party to that effect within such 20 day period, whereupon the other party may effect such a transfer within 30 days after the notice is given under Section 6(b) (i).

Any such transfer by a party under this Section 6(b) (ii) will be subject to and conditional upon the prior written consent of the other party, which consent will not be withheld if such other party's policies in effect at such time would permit it to enter into swap transactions with the transferee on the terms proposed.

(iii) Two Affected Parties. If an Illegality under Section 5(b) (i) (1) or a Tax Event occurs and there are two Affected Parties, each party will use all reasonable efforts to reach agreement within 30 days after notice thereof is given under Section 6(b) (i) on action that would cause such Termination Event to cease to exist.

(iv) Right to Terminate. If:

(1) a transfer under Section 6(b) (ii) or an agreement under Section 6(b) (iii), as the case may be, has not been effected with respect to all Affected Transactions within 30 days after an Affected Party gives notice under Section 6(b) (i); or

(2) an Illegality under Section 5(b) (i) (2) or a Credit Event Upon Merger occurs, or a Tax Event Upon Merger occurs and the Burdened Party is not the Affected Party, either party in the case of an Illegality, the Burdened Party in the case of a Tax Event Upon Merger, any Affected Party in the case of a Tax Event, or the party which is not the Affected Party in the case of a Credit Event Upon Merger, may, by not more than 20 days notice to the other party and provided that the relevant Termination Event is then continuing, designate a day not earlier than the day such notice is effective as an Early Termination Date in respect of all Affected Transactions.

(c) Effect of Designation.

(i) If notice designating an Early Termination Date is given under Section 6(a) or (b), the Early Termination Date will occur on the date so designated, whether or not the relevant Event of Default or Termination Event is continuing on the relevant Early Termination Date.

(ii) Upon the effectiveness of notice designating an Early Termination Date (or the deemed occurrence of an Early Termination Date), the obligations of the parties to make any further payments under Section 2(a) (i) in respect of the Terminated Transactions will terminate, but without prejudice to the other provisions of this Agreement.

(d) Calculations.

(i) Statement. Following the occurrence of an Early Termination Date, each party will make the calculations (including calculation of applicable interest rates) on its part contemplated by Section 6(e) and will provide to the other party a statement (1) showing, in reasonable detail, such calculations (including all relevant quotations) and (2) giving details of the relevant account to which any payment due to it under Section 6(e) is to be made. In the absence of written confirmation of a quotation obtained in determining a Market Quotation from the source providing such quotation, the records of the party obtaining such quotation will be conclusive evidence of the existence and accuracy of such quotation.

(ii) Due Date. The amount calculated as being payable under Section 6(e) will be due on the day that notice of the amount payable is effective (in the case of an Early Termination Date which is designated or deemed to occur as a result of an Event of Default) and not later than the day which is two Business Days after the day on which notice of the amount payable is effective (in the case of an Early Termination Date which is designated as a result of a Termination Event). Such amount will be paid together with (to the extent permitted under applicable law) interest thereon in the Termination Currency from (and including) the relevant Early Termination Date to (but excluding) the relevant due date, calculated as follows:

(1) if notice is given designating an Early Termination Date or if an Early Termination Date is deemed to occur, in either case as a result of an Event of Default, at the Default Rate; or

(2) if notice is given designating an Early Termination Date as a result of a Termination Event, at the Default Rate minus 1% per annum.

Such interest will be calculated on the basis of daily compounding and the actual number of days elapsed.

(e) Payments on Early Termination.

(i) Defaulting Party or One Affected Party. If notice is given designating an Early Termination Date or if an Early Termination Date is deemed to occur and there is a Defaulting Party or only one Affected Party, the other party will determine the Settlement Amount in respect of the Terminated Transactions and:

(1) if there is a Defaulting Party, the Defaulting Party will pay to the other party the excess, if a positive number, of (A) the sum of such Settlement Amount and the Termination Currency Equivalent of the Unpaid Amounts owing to the other party over (B) the Termination Currency Equivalent of the Unpaid Amounts owing to the Defaulting Party; and

(2) if there is an Affected Party, the payment to be made will be equal to (A) the sum of such Settlement Amount and the

Termination Currency Equivalent of the Unpaid Amounts owing to the party determining the Settlement Amount ('X') less (B) the Termination Currency Equivalent of the Unpaid Amounts owing to the party not determining the Settlement Amount ('Y').

(ii) Two Affected Parties. If notice is given of an Early Termination Date and there are two Affected parties, each party will determine a Settlement Amount in respect of the Terminated Transactions and the payment to be made will be equal to (1) the sum of (A) one-half of the difference between the Settlement Amount of the party with the higher Settlement Amount ('X') and the Settlement Amount of the party with the lower Settlement Amount ('Y') and (B) the Termination Currency Equivalent of the Unpaid Amounts owing to X less (2) the Termination Currency Equivalent of the Unpaid Amounts owing to Y.

(iii) Party Owing. If the amount calculated under Section 6(e) (i) (2) or (ii) is a positive number, Y will pay such amount to X; if such amount is a negative number, X will pay the absolute value of such amount to Y.

(iv) Adjustment for Bankruptcy. In circumstances where an Early Termination Date is deemed to occur, the amount determined under Section 6(e) (i) will be subject to such adjustments as are appropriate and permitted by law to reflect any payments made by one party to the other under this Agreement (and retained by such other party) during the period from the relevant Early Termination Date to the date for payment determined under Section 6(d) (ii).

(v) Pre-Estimate of Loss. The parties agree that the amounts recoverable under this Section 6(e) are a reasonable pre-estimate of loss and not a penalty. Such amounts are payable for the loss of bargain and the loss of protection against future risks and except as otherwise provided in this Agreement neither party will be entitled to recover any additional damages as a consequence of such losses.

7. Transfer

Subject to Section 6(b) and to any exception provided in the Schedule, neither this Agreement nor any interest or obligation in or under this Agreement may be transferred by either party without the prior written consent of the other party (other than pursuant to a consolidation or amalgamation with, or merger into, or transfer of all or substantially all its assets to, another entity) and any purported transfer without such consent will be void.

8. Contractual Currency

(a) Payment in the Contractual Currency. Each payment under this Agreement will be made in the relevant currency specified in this Agreement for that payment (the 'Contractual Currency'). To the extent permitted by applicable law, any obligation to make payments under this Agreement in the Contractual Currency will not be discharged or satisfied by any tender in any currency other than the Contractual Currency, except to the extent such tender results in the actual receipt by the party to which payment is owed, acting in a reasonable manner and in good faith in converting the currency so tendered into the Contractual Currency, of the full amount in the Contractual Currency of all amounts due in respect of this Agreement. If for any reason the amount in the Contractual Currency so received falls short of the amount in the Contractual Currency due in respect of this Agreement, the party required to make the payment will, to the extent permitted by applicable law, immediately pay such additional amount in the Contractual Currency as may be necessary to compensate for the shortfall. If for any reason the amount in the Contractual Currency so received exceeds the amount in the Contractual Currency due in respect of this Agreement, the party receiving the payment will refund promptly the amount of such excess.

(b) Judgments. To the extent permitted by applicable law, if any judgment or order expressed in a currency other than the Contractual Currency is rendered (i) for the payment of any amount owing in respect of this Agreement, (ii) for the payment of any amount relating to any early termination in respect of this Agreement or (iii) in respect of a judgment or order of another court for the payment of any amount described in (i) or (ii) above, the party seeking recovery, after recovery in full of the aggregate amount to which such party is entitled pursuant to the judgment or order, will be entitled to receive immediately from the other party the amount of any shortfall of the Contractual Currency received by such party as a consequence of sums paid in such other currency and will refund promptly to the other party any excess of the Contractual Currency received by such party as a consequence of sums paid in such other currency if such shortfall or such excess arises or results from any variation between the rate of exchange at which the Contractual Currency is converted into the currency of the judgment or order for the purpose of such judgment or order and the rate of exchange at which such party is able, acting in a reasonable manner and in good faith in converting the currency received into the Contractual Currency, to purchase the Contractual Currency with the amount of the currency of the judgment or order actually received by such party. The term 'rate of exchange' includes, without limitation, any premiums and costs of exchange payable in connection with the purchase of or conversion into the Contractual Currency.

(c) Separate Indemnities. To the extent permitted by applicable law, these indemnities constitute separate and independent obligations from the other obligations in this Agreement, will be enforceable as separate and independent causes of action, will apply notwithstanding any indulgence granted by the party to which any payment is owed and will not be affected by judgment being obtained or claim or proof being made for any other sums due in respect of this Agreement.

(d) Evidence of Loss. For the purpose of this Section 8, it will be sufficient for a party to demonstrate that it would have suffered a loss had an actual exchange or purchase been made.

9. Miscellaneous

(a) Entire Agreement. This Agreement constitutes the entire agreement and understanding of the parties with respect to its subject matter and supersedes all oral communication and prior writings with respect thereto.

(b) Amendments. No amendment, modification or waiver in respect of this Agreement will be effective unless in writing and executed by each of the parties or confirmed by an exchange of telexes.

(c) Survival of Obligations. Except as provided in Section 6(c) (ii), the obligations of the parties under this Agreement will survive the termination of any Swap Transaction.

(d) Remedies Cumulative. Except as provided in this Agreement, the rights, powers, remedies and privileges provided in this Agreement are cumulative and not exclusive of any rights, powers, remedies and privileges provided by law.

(e) Counterparts and Confirmations.

(i)   This Agreement may be executed in counterparts, each of which will be deemed an original.

(ii)   A Confirmation may be executed in counterparts or be created by an exchange of telexes, which in either case will be sufficient for all purposes to evidence a binding supplement to this

Agreement. Any such counterpart or telex will specify that it constitutes a Confirmation.

(f) No Waiver of Rights. A failure or delay in exercising any right, power or privilege in respect of this Agreement will not be presumed to operate as a waiver, and a single or partial exercise of any right, power or privilege will not be presumed to preclude any subsequent or further exercise of that right, power or privilege or the exercise of any other right, power or privilege.

(g) Headings. The headings used in this Agreement are for convenience of reference only and are not to affect the construction of or to be taken into consideration in interpreting this Agreement.

10. Multibranch Parties

If a party is specified as a Multibranch Party in Part 4 of the Schedule, such Multibranch Party may make and receive payments under any Swap Transaction through any of its branches or offices listed in the Schedule (each an 'Office'). The Office through which it so makes and receives payments for the purpose of any Swap Transaction will be specified in the relevant Confirmation and any change of Office for such purpose requires the prior written consent of the other party. Each Multibranch Party represents to the other party that, notwith-standing the place of payment, the obligations of each Office are for all purposes under this Agreement the obligations of such Multibranch Party. This representation will be deemed to be repeated by such Multibranch Party on each date on which a Swap Transaction is entered into.

11. Expenses

A Defaulting Party will, on demand, indemnify and hold harmless the other party for and against all reasonable out-of-pocket expenses, including legal fees and Stamp Tax, incurred by such other party by reason of the enforcement and protection of its rights under this Agreement or by reason of the early termination of any Swap Trans-action, including, but not limited to, costs of collection.

12. Notices

(a) Effectiveness. Any notice or communication in respect of this Agreement will be sufficiently given to a party if in writing and delivered in person, sent by certified or registered mail (airmail, if overseas) or the equivalent (with return receipt requested) or by overnight courier or given by telex (with answerback received) at the address or telex number specified in Part 4 of the Schedule. A notice or communication will be effective:

(i)   if delivered by hand or sent by overnight courier, on the day it is delivered (or if that day is not a day on which commercial banks are open for business in the city specified in the address for notice provided by the recipient (a 'Local Banking Day'), or if delivered after the close of business on a Local Banking Day, on the first following day that is a Local Banking Day);

(ii)   if sent by telex, on the day the recipient's answerback is received (or if that day is not a Local Banking Day, or if after the close of business on a Local Banking Day, on the first following day that is a Local Banking Day); or

(iii)   if sent by certified or registered mail (airmail, if overseas) or the equivalent (return receipt requested), three Local Banking Days after despatch if the recipient's address for notice is in the same country as the place of despatch and otherwise seven Local Banking Days after despatch.

(b) Change of Addresses. Either party may by notice to the other change the address or telex number at which notices or communications are to be given to it.

13. Governing Law and Jurisdiction

(a) Governing Law. This Agreement will be governed by and construed in accordance with the law specified in Part 4 of the Schedule.

(b) Jurisdiction. With respect to any suit, action or proceedings relating to this Agreement ('Proceedings'), each party irrevocably:

(i)   submits to the jurisdiction of the English courts, if this Agreement is expressed to be governed by English law, or to the non-exclusive jurisdiction of the courts of the State of New York and the United States District Court located in the Borough of Manhattan in New York City, if this Agreement is expressed to be governed by the laws of the State of New York; and

(ii)   waives any objection which it may have at any time to the laying of venue of any Proceedings brought in any such court, waives any claim that such Proceedings have been brought in an inconvenient forum and further waives the right to object, with respect to such Proceedings, that such court does not have jurisdiction over such party.

Nothing in this Agreement precludes either party from bringing Proceedings in any other jurisdiction (outside, if this Agreement is expressed to be governed by English law, the Contracting States, as defined in Section 1(3) of the Civil Jurisdiction and Judgments Act 1982 or any modification, extension or re-enactment thereof for the time being in force) nor will the bringing of Proceedings in any one or more jurisdictions preclude the bringing of Proceedings in any other jurisdiction.

(c) Service of Process. Each party irrevocably appoints the Process Agent (if any) specified opposite its name in Part 4 of the Schedule to receive, for it and on its behalf, service of process in any Proceedings. If for any reason any party's Process Agent is unable to act as such, such party will promptly notify the other party and within 30 days appoint a substitute process agent acceptable to the other party. The parties irrevocably consent to service of process given in the manner provided for notices in Section 12. Nothing in this Agreement will affect the right of either party to serve process in any other manner permitted by law.

(d) Waiver of Immunities. Each party irrevocably waives, to the fullest extent permitted by applicable law, with respect to itself and its revenues and assets (irrespective of their use or intended use), all immunity on the grounds of sovereignty or other similar grounds from (i) suit, (ii) jurisdiction of any court, (iii) relief by way of injunction, order for specific performance or for recovery of property, (iv) attachment of its assets (whether before or after judgment) and (v) execution or enforcement of any judgment to which it or its revenues or assets might otherwise be entitled in any Proceedings in the courts of any jurisdiction and irrevocably agrees, to the extent permitted by applicable law, that it will not claim any such immunity in any Proceedings.

14. Definitions

As used in this Agreement:

'Affected Party' has the meaning specified in Section 5(b).

'Affected Transactions' means (a) with respect to any Termination Event consisting of an Illegality, Tax Event or Tax Event Upon Merger, all Swap Transactions affected by the occurrence of such Termination Event and (b) with respect to any other Termination Event, all Swap Transactions.

'Affiliate' means, subject to Part 4 of the Schedule, in relation to any person, any entity controlled, directly or indirectly, by the person, any entity that controls, directly or indirectly, the person or any entity under common control with the person. For this purpose, 'control' of any entity or person means ownership of a majority of the voting power of the entity or person.

'Burdened Party' has the meaning specified in Section 5(b).

'Business Day' means (a) in relation to any payment due under Section 2(a) (i), a day on which commercial banks and foreign exchange markets are open for business in the place(s) specified in the relevant Confirmation and (b) in relation to any other payment, a day on which commercial banks and foreign exchange markets are open for business in the place where the relevant account is located and, if different, in the principal financial centre of the currency of such payment.

'Change in Tax Law' means the enactment, promulgation, execution or ratification of, or any change in or amendment to, any law (or in the application or official interpretation of any law) that occurs on or after the date on which the relevant Swap Transaction is entered into.

'consent' includes a consent, approval, action, authorization, exemption, notice, filing, registration or exchange control consent.

'Credit Event Upon Merger' has the meaning specified in Section 5(b).

'Credit Support Document' means any agreement or instrument which is specified as such in this Agreement.

'Default Rate' means a rate per annum equal to the cost (without proof or evidence of any actual cost) to the relevant payee (as certified by it) of funding the relevant amount plus 1% per annum.

'Defaulting Party' has the meaning specified in Section 6(a).

'Early Termination Date' means the date specified as such in a notice given under Section 6(a) or 6(b) (iv).

'Event of Default' has the meaning specified in Section 5(a).

'Illegality' has the meaning specified in Section 5(b).

'Indemnifiable Tax' means any Tax other than a Tax that would not be imposed in respect of a payment under this Agreement but for a present or former connection between the jurisdiction of the government or taxation authority imposing such Tax and the recipient of such payment or a person related to such recipient (including, without limitation, a connection arising from such recipient or related person being or having been a citizen or resident of such jurisdiction, or being or having been organized, present or engaged in a trade or business in such jurisdiction, or having had a permanent establishment or fixed place of business in such jurisdiction, but excluding a connection arising solely from such recipient or related person having executed, delivered, performed its obligations or received a payment under, or enforced, this Agreement or a Credit Support Document).

'law' includes any treaty, law, rule or regulation (as modified, in the case of tax matters, by the practice of any relevant governmental revenue authority) and

'lawful' and 'unlawful' will be construed accordingly.

'Loss' means, with respect to a Terminated Transaction and a party, an amount equal to the total amount (expressed as a positive amount) required, as determined as of the relevant Early Termination Date (or, if an Early Termination Date is deemed to occur, as of a time as soon thereafter as practicable) by the party in good faith, to compensate it for any losses and costs (including loss of bargain and costs of funding but excluding legal fees and other out-of-pocket expenses) that it may incur as a result of the early termination of the obligations of the parties in respect of such Terminated Transaction. If a party determines that it would gain or benefit from such early termination, such party's Loss will be an amount (expressed as a negative amount) equal to the amount of the gain or benefit as determined by such party.

'Market Quotation' means, with respect to a Terminated Transaction and a party to such Terminated Transaction making the determination, an amount (which may be negative) determined on the basis of quotations from Reference Market-makers for the amount that would be or would have been payable on the relevant Early Termination Date, either by the party to the Terminated Transaction making the determination (to be expressed as a positive amount) or to such party (to be expressed as a negative amount), in consideration of an agreement between such party and the quoting Reference Market-maker and subject to such documentation as they may in good faith agree, with the relevant Early Termination Date as the date of commencement of such agreement (or, if later, the date specified as the effective date of such Terminated Transaction in the relevant Confirmation), that would have the effect of preserving for such party the economic equivalent of the payment obligations of the parties under Section 2(a) (i) in respect of such Terminated Transaction that would, but for the occurrence of the relevant Early Termination Date, fall due after such Early Termination Date (excluding any Unpaid Amounts in respect of such Terminated Transaction but including, without limitation, any amounts that would, but for the occurrence of the relevant Early Termination Date, have been payable (assuming each applicable condition precedent had been satisfied) after such Early Termination Date by reference to any period in which such Early Termination Date occurs). The party making the determination (or its agent) will request each Reference Market-maker to provide its quotation to the extent practicable as of the same time (without regard to different time zones) on the relevant Early Termination Date (or, if an Early Termination Date is deemed to occur, as of a time as soon thereafter as practicable). The time as of which such quotations are to be obtained will, if only one party is obliged to make a determination under Section 6(e), be selected in good faith by that party and otherwise will be agreed by the parties. If more than three such quotations are provided, the Market Quotation will be the arithmetic mean of the Termination Currency Equivalent of the quotations, without regard to the quotations having the highest and lowest values. If exactly three such quotations are provided, the Market Quotation will be the quotation remaining after disregarding the quotations having the highest and lowest values. If fewer than three quotations are provided, it will be deemed that the Market Quotation in respect of such Terminated Transaction cannot be determined.

'Office' has the meaning specified in Section 10.

'Potential Event of Default' means any event which, with the giving of notice or the lapse of time or both, would constitute an Event of Default.

'Reference Market-makers' means four leading dealers in the relevant swap market selected by the party determining a Market Quotation in good faith (a) from among dealers of the highest credit standing which satisfy all the criteria that such party applies generally at the time in deciding whether to offer or to make an extension of credit and (b) to the extent practicable, from among such dealers having an office in the same city.

'Relevant jurisdiction' means, with respect to a party, the jurisdictions (a) in which the party is incorporated, organized, managed and controlled or considered to have its seat, (b) where a branch or office through which the party is acting for purposes of this Agreement is located, (c) in which the party executes this Agreement and (d) in relation to any payment, from or through which such payment is made.

'Scheduled Payment Date' means a date on which a payment is due under Section 2(a) (i) with respect to a Swap Transaction.

'Settlement Amount' means, with respect to a party and any Early Termination Date, the sum of:

(a) the Termination Currency Equivalent of the Market Quotations (whether positive or negative) for each Terminated Transaction for which a Market Quotation is determined; and

(b) for each Terminated Transaction for which a Market Quotation is not, or cannot be, determined, the Termination Currency Equivalent of such party's Loss (whether positive or negative); provided that if the parties agree that an amount may be payable under Section 6(e) to a Defaulting Party by the other party, no account shall be taken of a Settlement Amount expressed as a negative number.

'Specified Entity' has the meaning specified in Part 1 of the Schedule.

'Specified Indebtedness' means, subject to Part 1 of the Schedule, any obligation (whether present or future, contingent or otherwise, as principal or surety or otherwise) in respect of borrowed money.

'Specified Swap' means, subject to Part 1 of the Schedule, any rate swap or currency exchange transaction now existing or hereafter entered into between one party to this Agreement (or any applicable Specified Entity) and the other party to this Agreement (or any applicable Specified Entity).

'Stamp Tax' means any stamp, registration, documentation or similar tax.

'Tax' means any present or future tax, levy, impost, duty, charge, assessment or fee of any nature (including interest, penalties and additions thereto) that is imposed by any government or other taxing authority in respect of any payment under this Agreement other than a stamp, registration, documentation or similar tax.

'Tax Event' has the meaning specified in Section 5(b).

'Tax Event Upon Merger' has the meaning specified in Section 5(b).

'Terminated Transaction' means (a) with respect to any Early Termination Date occurring as a result of a Termination Event, all Affected Transactions and (b) with respect to any Early Termination Date occurring as a result of an Event of Default, all Swap Transactions, which in either case are in effect as of the time immediately preceding the effectiveness of the notice designating such Early Termination Date (or, in the case of an Event of Default specified in Section 5(a) (vii), in effect as of the time immediately preceding such Early Termination Date).

'Termination Currency' has the meaning specified in Part 1 of the Schedule.

'Termination Currency Equivalent' means, in respect of any amount denominated in the Termination Currency, such Termination Currency amount and, in respect of any amount denominated in a currency other than the Termination Currency (the 'Other Currency'), the amount in the Termination Currency determined by the party making the relevant determination as being required to purchase such amount of such Other Currency as at the relevant Early Termination Date with the Termination Currency at the rate equal to the spot exchange rate of the foreign exchange agent (selected as provided below) for the purchase of such Other Currency with the Termination Currency at or about 11.00 a.m. (in the city in which such foreign exchange agent is located) on such date as would be customary for the determination of such a rate for the purchase of such Other Currency for value the relevant Early Termination Date. The foreign exchange agent will, if only one party is obliged to make a determination under Section 6(e), be selected in good faith by that party and otherwise will be agreed by the parties.

'Termination Event' means an Illegality, a Tax Event, a Tax Event Upon Merger or a Credit Event Upon Merger.

'Unpaid Amounts' owing to any party means, with respect to any Early Termination Date, the aggregate of the amounts that became due and payable (or that would have become due and payable but for Section 2(a)(iii) or the designation or occurrence of such Early Termination Date) to such party under Section 2(a)(i) in respect of all Terminated Transactions by reference to all periods ended on or prior to such Early Termination Date and which remain unpaid as at such Early Termination Date, together with (to the extent permitted under applicable law and in lieu of any interest calculated under Section 2(e)) interest thereon, in the currency of such amounts, from (and including) the date such amounts became due and payable or would have become due and payable to (but excluding) such Early Termination Date, calculated as follows:

(a) in the case of notice of an Early Termination Date given as a result of an Event of Default:

(i)   interest on such amounts due and payable by a Defaulting Party will be calculated at the Default Rate; and

(ii)   interest on such amounts due and payable by the other party will be calculated at a rate per annum equal to the cost to such other party (as certified by it) if it were to fund such amounts (without proof or evidence of any actual cost); and

(b) in the case of notice of an Early Termination Date given as a result of a Termination Event, interest on such amounts due and payable by either party will be calculated at a rate per annum equal to the arithmetic mean of the cost (without proof or evidence of any actual cost) to each party (as certified by such party and regardless of whether due and payable by such party) if it were to fund or of funding such amounts.

Such amounts of interest will be calculated on the basis of daily compounding and the actual number of days elapsed.

IN WITNESS WHEREOF the parties have executed this document as of the date specified on the first page of this document.

....
(Name of party)   (Name of party)

By: ....   By: ....

Name: Name:

Title: Title:

APPENDIX III
GUIDE TO ISDA PUBLICATIONS

New in 1997

1996 ISDA Equity Derivatives Definitions

The 1996 Equity Derivatives Definitions are intended for use in confirmations of individual transactions governed by agreements such as the 1992 ISDA Master Agreement. The Definitions are primarily an expansion of the 1994 ISDA Equity Option Definitions, covering a wider range of basic transactions and variations. The purpose of these Definitions is to provide the basic framework for the documentation of an OT equity derivative transaction. Parties may find these Definitions a useful starting point when drafting a confirmation for a more exotic product-type.

EMU Continuity Provision

The provision is intended for use in existing and future ISDA Master Agreements where the parties wish to document their intention that European economic and monetary union (EMU) should not affect the continuity of their contract. The provision enables parties to confirm in their ISDA Master Agreement that EMU will not give either party the unilateral right to walk away from, or modify the terms of, any transaction governed by the agreement.

Standard Form Contracts

1992 ISDA Master Agreement (Multicurrency – Cross Border)

This agreement is used to document transactions between parties located in different jurisdictions and/or transactions involving different currencies. The Agreement is designed, among other things, to facilitate cross-product netting, and may be used to document a variety of derivative transactions. The 1992 agreements were prepared to accommodate transactions that could be documented under 1987 agreements with their 1989 and 1990 addenda. ISDA also prepared a User's Guide to assist in the understanding and use of this document.

1992 ISDA Master Agreement (Local Currency – Single Jurisdiction)

This agreement is used to document transactions between parties located in the same jurisdiction, and transactions involving one currency. The Agreement is designed, among other things, to facilitate cross-product netting, and may be used to document a wide variety of derivatives transactions. The 1992 agreements were prepared to accommodate transactions that could be documented under the 1987 agreements with their 1989 and 1990 addenda. ISDA also prepared a User's Guide to assist in the understanding and use of this document.

1994 Credit Support Annex (Subject to New York Law Only)

This annex allows parties to establish bilateral mark-to-market security arrangements. This document serves as an annex to the schedule to the Master Agreements and is designed for use in transactions subject to New York law. ISDA also prepared a User's Guide to assist in the understanding and use of this annex.

1995 Credit Support Deed (Security Interest – English Law)

This deed allows parties to establish bilateral mark-to-market collateral arrangements under English law relying on creation of a formal security interest in collateral in the form of securities and/or cash. It is a stand-alone document (not an annex to the Schedule), but is otherwise comparable to the 1994 ISDA Credit Support Annex for use with ISDA Master Agreements subject to New York law (which also relies on creation of a formal security interest in the collateral).

1995 Credit Support Annex (Transfer – English Law)

This annex allows parties to establish bilateral mark-to-market arrangements under English law relying on transfer of title to collateral in the form of securities and/or cash and, in the event of default, inclusion of collateral values within the close-out netting provided by Section 6 of the ISDA Master Agreement. The Credit Support Annex does not create a security interest, but instead relies on netting for its effectiveness. Like the New York form, it is an annex to the Schedule to the ISDA Master Agreement.

1995 Credit Support annex (Security Interest – Japanese Law)

This annex was prepared for use in documenting bilateral security and other credit support arrangements between counterparties for transactions documented under an ISDA Master Agreement for which the parties intend to use assets located in Japan as credit support. This Annex assumes that Japanese law will govern questions of perfection and priorities relating to Posted Collateral, and is designed to provide documentation for parties wishing to minimize exposure to counterparties through collateral arrangements in respect of cash, deposit accounts, Japanese government bonds or other marketable securities situated in Japan. The structure and wording of this Annex were designed to conform to the 1994 ISDA Credit Support Annex in order to facilitate its use by those familiar with the 1994 Annex. Therefore, parties should generally refer to the User's Guide to the 1994 Credit Support Annex. The User's Guide to the Japanese law Annex discusses the differences between the 1994 Annex and the 1995 Japanese Annex.

1992 US Municipal Counterparty Schedule

This schedule is for US counterparties entering into transactions with US municipal counterparties. The Schedule contains various customized provisions for the documentation of transactions with US municipal counterparties under the 1992 Master Agreement (Local Currency – Single Jurisdiction). This document is sold with the 1992 US Municipal Counterparty Definitions.

1992 Confirmation for OTC Equity Index Option Transactions

This confirmation is designed to facilitate the documentation of certain equity derivative transactions under the ISDA Master Agreement.

1993 Confirmation of OTC Bond Option Transactions

This confirmation is designed to facilitate the documentation of bond option transactions that settle by delivery or for cash settled bond options.

1994 Confirmation of OTC Single Share Option Transactions (Physical Settlement)

This confirmation is designed to facilitate the documentation of single share option transactions that settle by physical delivery.

1994 Amendment to the 1987 Interest Rate Swap Agreement to Provide for Full Two-Way Payments

This amendment is designed to assist in converting outstanding

1987 Agreements from limited two-way payments to full two-way payments.

1994 Amendment to the 1987 Interest Rate & Currency Exchange Agreement to Provide for Full Two-Way Payments

This amendment is designed to assist in converting outstanding 1987 Agreements from limited two-way payments to full two-way payments.

1987 Interest Rate Swap Agreement

The agreement is used to document US dollar-denominated interest rate swaps. It is intended for use with the 1986 Code and incorporates it by reference. The 1992 Master Agreements were prepared to accommodate transactions that could be documented under the 1987 agreements with their 1989 and 1990 addenda, as well as other types of OTC derivatives.

1987 Interest Rate and Currency Exchange Agreement

This agreement is used to document currency swaps and interest rate swaps in 15 currencies (include US dollars). It does not incorporate the 1986 Code, but contains substantially identical provisions. The 1991 Definitions were developed for use with this agreement. In 1991 ISDA authorized a project to revise this agreement and related documentation. This project resulted in the publication of the 1992 Master Agreements and several product-specific definitional booklets and forms of confirmations.

1989 Addenda to ISDA Schedules for Interest Rate Caps, Collars & Floors

This addenda enables swap counterparties to include caps, collars and floors and similar products under the 1987 Agreements. A Commentary on the use of the Addenda is included. The necessary provisions for documenting these transactions are included in the 1992 agreements and 1991 Definitions (except those provisions noted in the 1992 User's Guide to the Master Agreements).

1990 Addenda to ISDA Schedules for Options

This addenda enables swap counterparties to include option transactions under the 1987 agreements. A Commentary on the use of the Addenda is included. The necessary provisions for documenting these transactions are included in the 1991 agreements and 1991 Definitions (except those provisions noted in the 1992 User's Guide to the Master Agreements).

1995 Standard Terms and Conditions for Escrow Float Transactions

These standard terms and conditions are intended for use in connection with escrow float transactions involving the investment at one or more future dates by a trustee or escrow agent, in government securities, of the principal and interest proceeds of securities held by the trustee in trust or escrow to effect the repayment of bonds. The standard terms and related agreements into which they may be incorporated provide means to provide the trustee fixed returns from its investment of such principal and interest proceeds from the date of their receipt until the date they are needed to make bond payments.

1996 Representation Regarding Relationship Between Parties

This Representation Regarding Relationship Between Parties may be used in existing and future ISDA Master Agreements where the parties wish to document their understanding of the nature of their relationship. The relationship described in the representation is the one most frequently encountered in the wholesale financial markets. The representation should be included only when it accurately reflects how the parties are acting, their capabilities and the nature of their relationship.

1996 ISDA/BBAIRS Bridge and ISDA/FRABBA Bridge

The contractual provisions contained in this document create a bridge between the 1987 or 1992 ISDA Master Agreements and swap transactions entered into using BBAIRS terms or forward rate agreements entered into using FRABBA terms.

Guides and Definitional Booklets

User's Guide to the 1992 ISDA Master Agreements

This manual is designed to assist in the understanding and use of the *1992 ISDA Master Agreements*, definitional booklets, and forms confirmation. This publication provides a detailed, section-by-section review of the provisions featured in the *1992 Master Agreements* and how they differ from those published in 1987, as well as tax matters, issues relating to set-off, and new technologies. Translations of the *User's Guide* are available in Simplified and Traditional Chinese.

Traditional Chinese Character Translation of the User's guide to the ISDA Master Agreement
Simplified Chinese Character Translation of the User's Guide to the ISDA Master Agreement

These translations of the *User's Guide* to the *1992 ISDA Master* Agreements in simplified and traditional Chinese are intended to assist in the understanding and use of the *1992 ISDA Master Agreements*, definitional booklets, and forms of confirmation. These publications provide a review of the provisions featured in the *1992 Master Agreement* and how they differ from those published in 1987, as well as tax matters, issues relating to set-off, and new technologies.

User's Guide to the 1994 ISDA Credit Support Annex

This manual is designed to assist in the understanding and use of the *1994 ISDA Credit Support Annex (Subject to New York Law Only)* which is used in documenting bilateral security and other credit support arrangements between counterparties for transactions documented under a Master Agreement that selects New York law as the governing law.

User's Guide to the 1995 ISDA Credit Support Annex (Security Interest – Japanese Law)

This manual discusses the differences between the *1994 ISDA Credit Support Annex (Subject to New York Law)* and the *1995 Japanese Law Credit Support Annex*. The structure and wording of the *1995 Japanese Law Annex* were designed to conform to the *1994 ISDA Credit Support Annex (Subject to New York Law)* in order to facilitate its use by those familiar with the 1994 Annex. Therefore, parties should generally refer to the *User's Guide to the 1994 Credit Support Annex*.

1992 US Municipal Counterparty Definitions

These definitions are designed to facilitate the documentation of interest rate swap transactions with US municipal counterparties. Sample forms of confirmation are included. This document is sold with the *US Municipal Counterparty Schedule*.

1992 FX and Currency Option Definitions

These definitions are designed to facilitate the documentation of FX and currency option transactions under the *1992 Master Agreement (Multicurrency – Cross Border)*. Sample forms of confirmation are included.

1993 ISDA Commodity Derivatives Definitions

These definitions are designed to facilitate the documentation of commodity transactions under the 1992 Master Agreements. Sample forms of confirmation are included.

1994 ISDA Equity Option Definitions

These definitions are intended for use with the 1992 Master Agreements and confirmations of individual transactions governed by those agreements. The Definitions reflect the terms of the two long-form confirmations (*1992 OTC Equity Index Option Confirmation* and *1994 OTC Single Share Option Transaction Confirmation*) and include a short-form confirmation for participants in the markets for OTC equity option transactions to document OTC equity index and physically settled single-share option transactions. The *1996 ISDA Equity Derivatives Definitions* cover a wider range of transactions than the *1994 ISDA Equity Option Definitions*.

1991 ISDA Definitions

These definitions are intended for use with the *1987 ISDA Interest rate and Currency Exchange Agreement* and *1992 ISDA Master Agreement (Multi-Currency)*. The Definitions provide a set of standard terms, including floating-rate options, and the basis for calculating fixed and floating amounts, for incorporation in each transaction confirmation under the multi-currency documents. The 1991 Definitions are an expansion of the *1987 Interest Rate and Currency Exchange Definitions* and include new definitions, additional currencies, certain provisions from the 1989 and 1990 addenda, and exhibits depicting forms of telex or letter agreement that may be used as a confirmation for individual transactions.

1987 User's Guide to the Standard Form Agreements

This guide describes how the 1987 agreements can be used to document interest rate swaps, currency swaps and cross-currency interest rate swaps. The Guide provides an overview of how to use the two forms, which differ principally in the type of transactions to which each is suited. The *User's Guide* also contains a section-by-section description of the provisions contained in the Agreements. The Guide highlights items parties must complete, optional provisions, and the use of the *1986 Code* and *1987 Interest Rate and Currency Exchange Definitions* in conjunction with the 1987 agreements.

1986 Code of Standard Wording, Assumptions and Provisions for Swaps

This code represents ISDA's initial effort to standardize and simplify documentation for US dollar-denominated interest rate swaps. The Code covers subjects as diverse as compounding of floating amounts, default and termination events, standard representations and covenants, and cross-border and tax-related matters.

GLOSSARY

Amortizing swap A swap in which the notional principal is reduced by an agreed amount each period over the life of the swap.

Asset swap A swap which is coupled with a bond in order to change the structure of the bond. The bond may already be held in the investor's portfolio, or it may be bought together with the swap as a package.

Assignment When a new counterparty replaces one of the original counterparties on a swap.

Basis risk The risk that there will be a divergence between two markets, for example, LIBOR and Eurodollar futures.

Basis swap A floating-floating swap, for example LIBOR-LIBOR, Prime-LIBOR, CP-LIBOR.

Bullet maturity A bond which pays interest periodically, and repays the principal upon maturity.

Callable In the case of a bond, it is the right of the issuer to buy the bonds back from the investor. In the case of a swap, it is the right of the fixed-rate payer to cancel the swap.

Cap An instrument purchased to set a ceiling on the interest rate payable by a borrower.

Cedel One of the two major Eurobond clearing systems in Europe.

Collar A position which is made up of a long cap and a short floor.

Commodity swap A swap in which the floating rate is linked to the price of a specific commodity such as wheat or gold.

Comparative advantage When a firm has the capacity to borrow funds in a particular market at a preferential rate.

Convexity The curvilinear price/yield relationship which can be used in establishing a hedge ratio.

Credit risk The risk that the swap counterparty will default on its obligations.

Currency swap When interest rate payments denominated in one currency are exchanged for interest rate payments denominated in another currency.

Debt warrant An option to purchase more bonds on fixed terms at the time of the offering of the warrants.

Decompounded rate A scaled-down rate used for a shorter period or 'stub' in a swap. This is normally only used in the US dollar market.

Dual currency bond   A bond which pays interest in one currency and repays the principal in another currency.

Duration   The weighted average of the time when payments are made on an instrument. It measures the price volatility of an instrument for a given change in yield.

Equity-linked bond   When the investor has the privilege of converting the bonds into shares.

Euroclear   One of the two major Eurobond clearing systems in Europe.

Floor   An instrument purchased to set a minimum return receivable by an investor.

Forward swap   A swap which starts at some point in the future.

Futures strip   A stream or series of short-term futures contracts which when grossed up will generate a return for a term equal to the length of the strip.

Generic swap   Also known as a 'plain vanilla' swap, this swap involves the exchange of periodic payments calculated on a fixed-rate basis for periodic payments calculated on a floating-rate basis.

Interest rate swap   Periodic payments calculated on one basis on a notional principal are exchanged for periodic payments calculated on another basis in the same currency.

Intermediary   A bank or financial institution which puts two swap counterparties together for a fee.

Interpolate   To estimate between the values already known or determined.

ISDA   International Swaps and Derivatives Association.

Liability swap   A swap which is coupled with a bond in order to change the structure of the bond. The bond may already have been issued by the borrower or it may be issued together with the swap as a package.

LIBOR-in-arrears swap   A swap in which LIBOR is set usually two days prior to the payment date.

Mismatch risk   The risk which arises in a swap portfolio when the terms of two offsetting swaps do not exactly match, for example, a mismatch between 3- and 6-month LIBOR.

Modified duration   A figure derived from the duration of an instrument which measures the price volatility of an instrument for a given change in yield.

Off-market coupon swap   A swap in which the coupon is above or below the current market value.

Par yield curve   A curve which measures yield over time.

Parallel loan   The forerunner of the swap. Two companies based in different countries would lend each other funds denominated in their domestic currency, and interest payments would be made on the nominal principal.

Participation swap   A transaction which operates as a cap on a full notional principal if LIBOR is set above the agreed interest rate and operates as a swap on a portion of the notional principal if LIBOR is set below the agreed interest rate.

Payer   The payer in the swap is the counterparty which pays the fixed rate and receives the floating rate.

Portfolio   A list of swaps currently being held by an institution.

Present value of a basis point   The change in the price of an instrument for a 1 basis point change in yield.

Putable   In the case of a bond, it is the right of the investor to sell the bond back to the issuer. In the case of a swap, it is the right of the fixed-rate receiver to cancel the swap.

Quality spread differential   The premium a weaker credit must pay over a stronger credit when raising funds of the same denomination and maturity.

Receiver   The receiver in the swap is the counterparty which receives the fixed rate and pays the floating rate.

Resettable coupon   A bond which allows the issuer to reset the coupon midway through the life of the bond.

Retractable coupon   A bond which allows the investor to sell the bonds back to the issuer at par if the new fixed rate on a resettable coupon bond is unacceptable.

Roller-coaster swap   A swap in which the notional principal increases and decreases by an agreed amount each period over the life of the swap.

Sinking fund   A bond which requires the issuer to redeem a part of the principal on an amortizing basis.

Step-down coupon   A bond which begins its life carrying a coupon above the current market rates, but periodically, the coupon is reduced so that in the later years the coupon is set below current market levels.

Step-up coupon   A bond which begins its life carrying a coupon below the current market rates, but periodically, the coupon is increased so that in the later years the coupon is set above current market levels.

Swap spread   The difference between the bid and offered side of the swap. Can also refer to the spread over treasuries – that is, the difference between the yield on the treasury note and the bid or offer on the swap.

Swaption   An option to pay or receive in a swap.

Synthetic instrument   When an instrument's structure is changed to simulate another instrument. For example, an asset swap may change a fixed-rate bond into a synthetic floating-rate instrument.

Termination   The cancellation of a swap.

Theoretical spot rate   The rate used as a discount factor to derive the zero-coupon yield curve.

Warehouse   A swap portfolio held by a market-maker. The market-maker may enter into a swap and put it in the warehouse until a suitable counterparty can be found.

Zero-coupon yield curve   When the theoretical spot rates are constructed as a curve to show yield over time.

INDEX